Designing Clothes with the Flat Pattern Method

Brimming with creative inspiration, how-to projects, and useful information to enrich your everyday life, quarto.com is a favorite destination for those pursuing their interests and passions.

ISBN: 978-1-58923-934-0

Library of Congress Cataloging-in-Publication Data

Names: Alm, Sara, author.
Title: Designing clothes with the flat pattern method : customize fitting shells to create garments in any style / Sara Alm.
Description: Minneapolis, MN : Creative Publishing International, 2017.
Identifiers: LCCN 2016056502 | ISBN 9781589239340 (paperback)
Subjects: LCSH: Dressmaking--Pattern design. | BISAC: CRAFTS & HOBBIES / Fashion. | CRAFTS & HOBBIES / Sewing. | DESIGN / Fashion.
Classification: LCC TT520 .A4365 2017 | DDC 646.4--dc23
LC record available at https://lccn.loc.gov/2016056502

Design: Timothy Samara
Cover Image: Ken Gutmaker
Photography: Ken Gutmaker
Illustration: Sara Alm

Designing Clothes with the Flat Pattern Method

SARA ALM

Customize Fitting Shells to Create Garments in Any Style

Creative Publishing
international

Contents

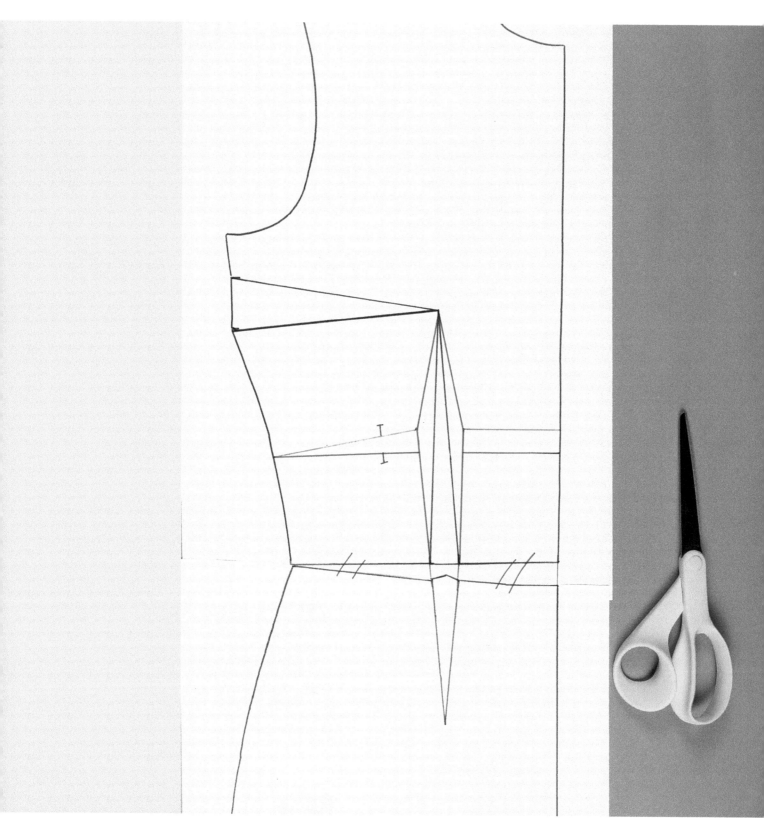

I have always loved creating and designing clothing; it is a fun way to express myself. Sewing from commercial patterns gave me a great start, but it left me wanting more. I found myself yearning to adjust patterns, alter clothing from my wardrobe, and experiment with new ideas. I fell in love with patternmaking.

Designing clothes with the flat pattern method gave me the ability to create endless possibilities of silhouettes from basic styles. It is easy to make a simple garment pattern into a block or master pattern. I am excited to share techniques that will enable you to realize your own designs, ones that speak to you, about you, and for you. Find your inspiration anywhere, and let this book guide you to create new designs.

Only very basic tools are needed to begin designing clothes with the flat pattern method. Creating your own designs will be rewarding if you possess garment sewing knowledge, imagination, and a sense of adventure. A great-fitting master pattern is a critical first step. First read Chapter 1, Master Pattern Basics, so you have a great foundation, and then dive into the sections that intrigue you the most.

The step-by-step instructions will show you techniques to create certain styles, but I encourage you to mix and match techniques, try them on different areas of a garment than I have shown, and even try to break some rules. Although not every pattern you create will be a success, you will learn so much from it and hopefully have fun in the exploration

Sara Alm

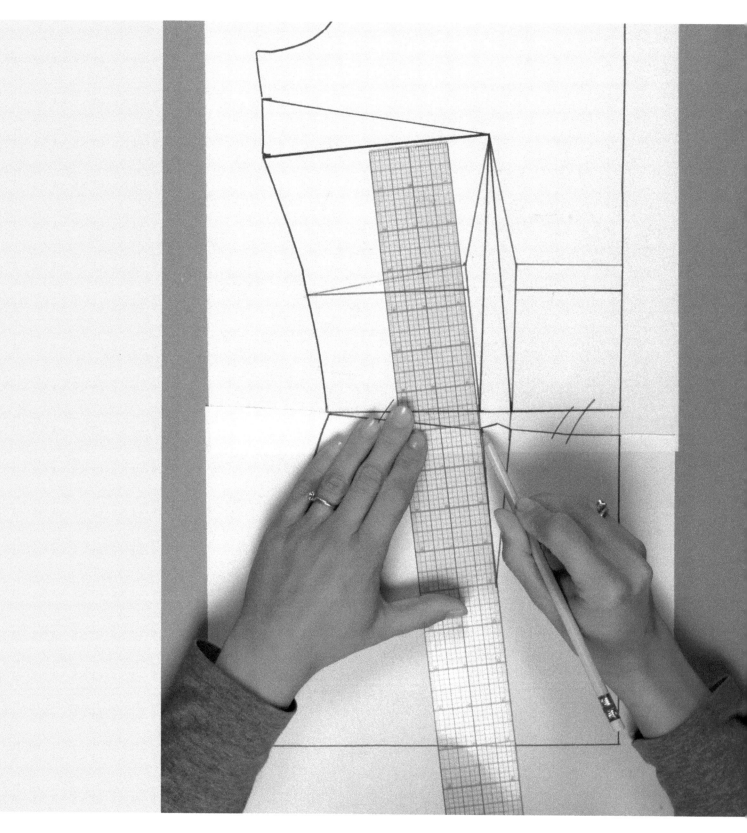

Master Pattern Basics

This chapter covers which patterns make good master patterns and how to ready them for the design process.

What Is a Master Pattern?

A garment that fits well and has virtually no design details at all makes a great foundation pattern or master pattern. The beauty of this simple blank template is that new stylelines, silhouettes, and design details can be applied to it. Fitting shells are available from commercial pattern companies like Vogue and Butterick. There are also companies that provide custom sizing services; Pattern String Codes is one such company. You could have as few as four basic master patterns: skirt, bodice, sleeve, and pant. But as you create garments of similar styles or silhouettes, you can grow a whole library of master patterns: blouse, jacket, sleeveless dress, wide-leg pant, and more.

Although fitting shells are a true foundation, really any well-fitting garment can become a starting point for your design. If you have a garment pattern that you love the fit of and can imagine creating stylistic variations of it over and over again, then use that pattern to create a master pattern. That said, the most versatile master patterns are still the most basic garments, without many stylelines or design details. Any master pattern should be simplified down to darts instead of stylelines and stripped of pockets, yokes, cuffs, and zipper and button extensions—the simpler the garment, the better. Princess seamline dresses and jackets can be turned into master patterns. Tops with jewel necklines, basic sleeves, and hems that fall straight down from the hip are the best. All different styles of pants, from fitted to relaxed, make great pant masters. You must make sure the fit is great to start. If you use an ill-fitted master, each and every one of your designs will also suffer from ill fit.

Setting Up and Using Master Patterns

Once you have a great-fitting base pattern, make it a master. Spend the quality time getting the fit right; all future designs will benefit from it.

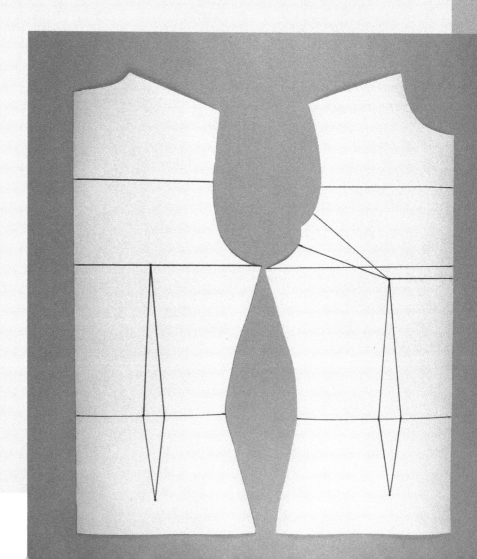

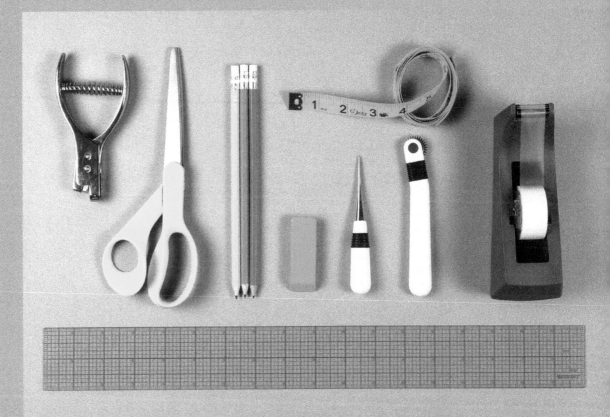

Paper
The paper you use for your master
pattern will be used over and over
again, so be sure to copy the pattern
onto a heavyweight paper. Oak tag,
which is very similar to what manila
file folders are made from, is used in
the apparel industry. Oak tag can be
found at online suppliers and many
fabric stores. Chipboard and poster
board are also suitable materials.
The goal is to have a paper that is easy
to trace around the edges and holds
up to some abuse.

The paper you use for pattern drafting
should be lightweight, white, and
ideally come on a roll. It is great if it
folds easily and you can see through
it to trace pattern pieces. There are
many suitable papers available from
art supply stores as well as apparel
industry suppliers.

GUIDELINES

Depending on what type of master pattern you are setting up—skirt, bodice, sleeve, or pant—you will have many guidelines. Well-marked darts and guidelines are critical for purposes of design and fit. Important guidelines are listed below. If your patterns do not already have these guidelines, follow the instructions below to position them correctly.

Cross front and back Horizontal guideline below your neck and shoulder perpendicular to the center front or back. It connects the center to the armhole before it begins to curve to the side seam.

Bust Horizontal guideline perpendicular to the center front or back. It connects the center to the base of the armhole at the side seam.

Waist Horizontal guideline perpendicular to the center front or back at the smallest part of your body and where your darts are the fullest. On a skirt or pant, the guideline is the top of the pattern and may be curved.

Bust apex An awl punch at the fullest point of the bust. It is often marked on commercial patterns, but be sure to mark its location on your body in a fitting.

Bust apex guideline Horizontal guideline perpendicular to the center front that connects to your bust apex.

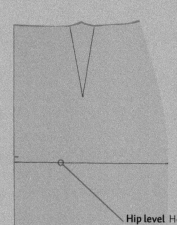

Quarter lines Vertically oriented guidelines connecting the sleeve cap to the base.

Bicep Horizontal guideline that connects the underarm seam of the sleeve front to the back underarm seam, the fullest part of the sleeve.

Elbow Horizontal guideline parallel to the base of the sleeve at the level of your elbow. This is easiest to mark while wearing a fitting shell.

Hip level Horizontal guideline at the fullest point below the waist perpendicular to the center front or back; it connects the center to the side seam. Again, it is often marked on commercial patterns, but make sure it is where you are fullest (it may be higher or lower).

Base Horizontal guideline at the bottom of the pattern. This should be placed at your favorite length for that garment.

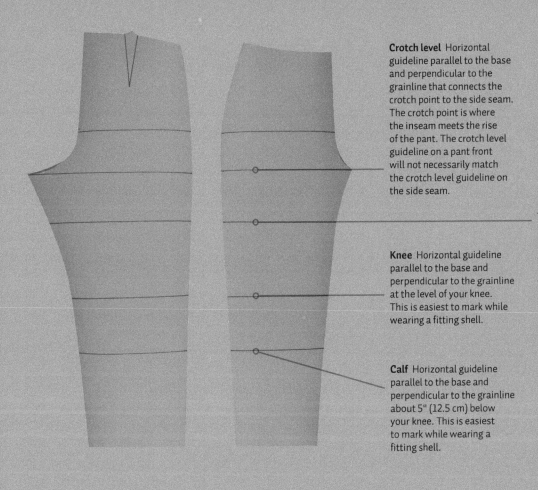

Crotch level Horizontal guideline parallel to the base and perpendicular to the grainline that connects the crotch point to the side seam. The crotch point is where the inseam meets the rise of the pant. The crotch level guideline on a pant front will not necessarily match the crotch level guideline on the side seam.

Thigh Horizontal guideline parallel to the base and perpendicular to the grainline about 7" (17.8 cm) above your knee. This is easiest to mark while wearing a fitting shell.

Knee Horizontal guideline parallel to the base and perpendicular to the grainline at the level of your knee. This is easiest to mark while wearing a fitting shell.

Calf Horizontal guideline parallel to the base and perpendicular to the grainline about 5" (12.5 cm) below your knee. This is easiest to mark while wearing a fitting shell.

Measurements

Write your measurements on each guideline of your master pattern. Do not include dart take-up. For example, if your front waist guideline measures 8 inches (20.3 cm) and has a 1-inch (2.5 cm) dart that intersects it, your waist measurement is 7 inches (17.8 cm).

These measurements include ease. Calculate how much ease exists on each guideline. Measure your body's full circumference on any given guideline while wearing your master pattern so you are measuring on the guideline.

Master pattern measurement	Front	+	Back	=	Multiply by	=	−	Full body measurement	= Total amount of ease	Divide by	= Amount of ease per pattern piece
Sample Waist	8" (20.3 cm)		7½" (19 cm)	15½" (39.4 cm)	x2	31" (76.2 cm)		30" (76.2 cm)	1" (2.5 cm)	÷4	¼" (6 mm)
Waist					x2					÷4	
Hip Level					x2					÷4	
Bust					x2					÷4	
Knee										÷2	
Thigh										÷2	
Bicep										÷2	
Elbow										÷2	

Making Your Master Pattern

Take your paper pattern with all the guidelines, seamlines, and darts drawn in and secure it to the oak tag or similar board with tape. Press firmly with a tracing wheel to transfer your seamlines, darts, and guidelines onto the template paper, excluding seam allowance. The tracing wheel will leave a dotted impression, then draw over that with pen or pencil. Cut out your template.

Check that the front and back are the same length at the sides and shoulder seams only, and remember that darts may intersect these seamlines. Also check that the bust, waist, hip level, thigh, knee, and hem guidelines match up along the sides. Adjust the guidelines as necessary to match.

Use a notcher to notch your guidelines and dart legs on the perimeter of the master pattern. If you do not have a notcher, make shallow and narrow triangular cutouts of your guidelines and dart legs on the perimeter of your template paper. Use an awl punch to pierce the dart points, the dart take-up in the interior of the pattern piece, and the bust apex. The notches (or cutouts) and awl punches will be used to mark guidelines as you begin to design your new patterns.

The master pattern should be kept flat or hung from a pattern hook so its shape does not become distorted.

Seam Allowance

The master pattern should *not* include any seam allowance. This will take a little getting used to. Since all pattern pieces are "working patterns" while you are in the design process, all will need seam allowance added to them. Errors can pop up while sewing if you have inadvertently added seam allowance to parts of your pattern while drafting it. It is easier to make adjustments to the fit and create new stylelines without seam allowance. Make sure you have your seamlines drawn on your foundation pattern pieces. If you are using a commercial pattern, the seamlines would be less the seam allowance indicated on the pattern, generally ⅝" (1.5 cm) from the pattern edge.

Although they are not exactly seamlines, button and zipper extensions that are commonly built beyond the center front or center back guidelines should be excluded from all master patterns. Unless you plan to finish every new design with the same size and type of closure, remove the button and zipper extensions.

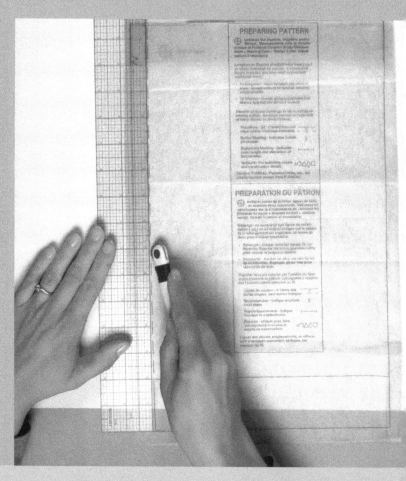

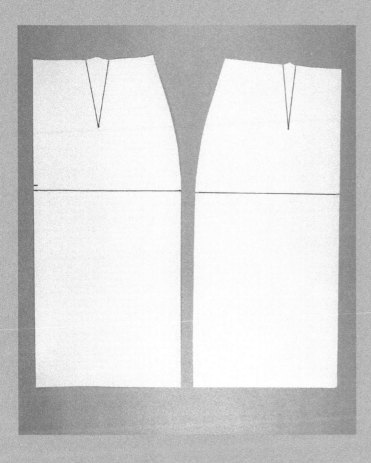

Adding Ease

As mentioned earlier, your fitting shell or master pattern should be quite fitted in order for it to be a good base. However, not every garment should fit and feel the same way. Adding extra ease will make certain garments feel more comfortable and look more relaxed.

One way of doing this is to ignore waist darts or use only a small portion of the dart take-up. This can make a great difference in the bodice of tops and dresses. In all other garments, extra ease can be added to the side seams, and this can be done in addition to ignoring darts or not. A jacket or coat commonly has an extra 2 inches (5.1 cm) of ease than just a blouse. To do this, just add ½ inch (1.3 cm) to the side seams of both the front and the back of the garment.

Changing the armhole can also make a more relaxed-fitting garment. I do love a high armhole because it can actually give you a wide range of motion, assuming you can sew a well-fitted sleeve into the armhole. But it is not so comfortable when wearing something underneath a coat. Follow this general rule for the armhole: lower your armhole only by the amount of ease you have added to that pattern piece. If, for example, you have added an extra ½-inch (1.3 cm) ease to your garment, then you can lower your armhole ½ inch (1.3 cm). Be sure to do this to both the front and the back. Also, you will need to measure your armhole and make changes to your sleeve, as it too will need to get bigger.

How to Use Your Master Pattern

Now that you have set up your master pattern, begin drafting!

Place any lightweight white paper that comes on a roll under your master pattern. With a pencil, trace around your master pattern, dipping your pencil into each notch and awl punch. Connect your notches on guidelines and notches to awl punches for darts. Follow any of the drafting exercises that intrigue you [A].

Working Pattern

After you have flat patterned a new design, you are still "working" on it because you need to fit your new design! Do not assume that a great-fitting master pattern will produce perfectly fitting new designs. New designs need to be sewn in muslin without any finishing details for fit testing [B].

Seam allowance needs to be added to your working pattern because your master pattern is set up without it. You can do this either on the paper pattern or on the fabric as you are cutting it out. My preference is to add the seam allowance to the fabric only. It is easier to adjust your working paper pattern without seam allowance because you will be making changes directly to your seamlines as opposed to your seam allowance [C],[D].

[A]

[B]

Final Pattern

Once the fitting is successful, make it a final pattern. A final pattern can be made of either oak tag or drafting paper. Your choice of paper depends on how many times you plan to make this particular garment. An oak tag pattern will last much longer, though it is less storage friendly. The final pattern should have seam allowance all the way around the edges, excluding edges to be placed on the fold. Bring your notches to the new edge of the paper. Remember to mark all darts, grainlines, cutting instructions, pattern name, and pattern piece name [E].

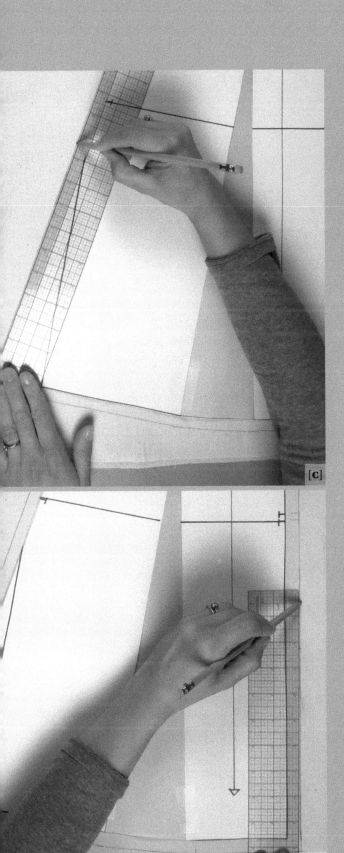

[C]

[D]

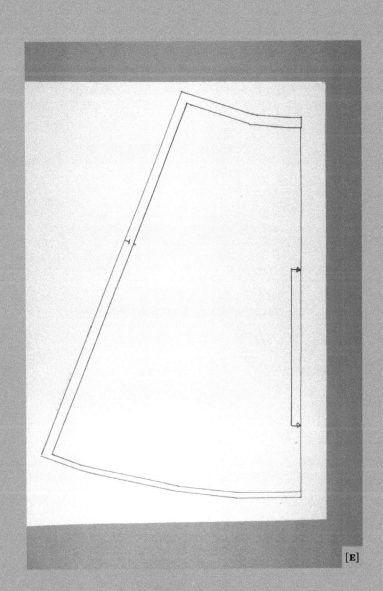

[E]

Skirts

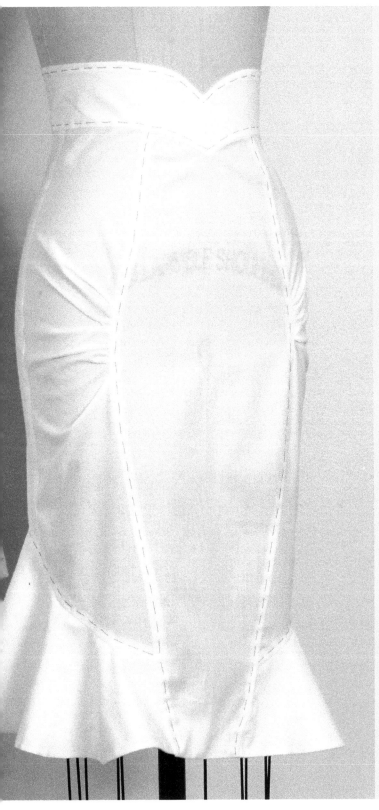

Skirts are a great way to begin learning the flat pattern method. By combining different options that are presented in the Skirts chapter, you will be able to design an endless array of styles and silhouettes. There are fewer obstacles and little shaping in the way of darts, making the drafting less complicated (unlike the bodice).

———

The flat patterning techniques that are used in skirts are universal and can be applied to all garment types.

Changes to the Waistline

Before drafting any other part of your skirt, decide on your waistline placement and finish.

Waistline options include raising or lowering the waistline. Many commercial patterns are designed to fit at the natural waistline, at or near the navel. Since this may not be the most comfortable or flattering position for you, changes can be made.

In addition to where your waistline is, you have several finish options, including a straight or contoured waistband, a facing, or a yoke.

Before drafting, take two measurements to change the position of your waistline, whether you raise or lower it.

1

While wearing your sewn skirt-fitting muslin, measure the distance between the original waist and the desired new waist position.

2

Measure the circumference of your body at this new waistline position.

3

Add ½" (1.3 cm) ease for a raised waistline skirt. Add no ease to a lowered waistline skirt.

4

Subtract the difference between your new adjusted waistline circumference, plus ease, and your total master pattern waistline (this is your front and back excluding darts multiplied by 2). If this number is negative, your raised waistline is smaller than your waist.

5

Divide the difference by 4. This is the adjustment you will make on both your front and your back new waistline. Round this number to the nearest ⅛" increment or nearest millimeter.

Lowered Waistline

For a lowered waistline skirt, the adjustment can be as little as ½ inch (1.3 cm) below your original waist. The limitation to how low you go is really dependent on the curve of your body. If your body is relatively straight from waist to hip level, or the difference between your waist and your low hip circumference is small, your skirt may fall off if you lower the waistline too much. If your body's shape is curvy from waist to hip, you may be able to lower your waistline more. Regardless of the shape of your body, a good reference point is the side seams of your favorite lowered waistline pants.

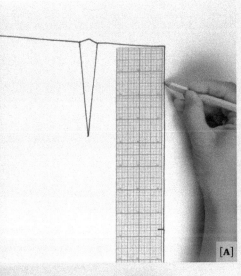

[A]

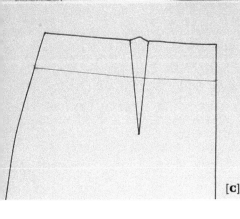

[B]

[C]

1

Trace your front skirt master pattern onto drafting paper.

2

On the center front, measure down from the waistline the desired depth of your new waistline [A]. Do the same along the side seam [B].

3

Draw in a new waistline shape connecting the two points. Make the curve similar to the original waistline shape [C].

4

Measure along the new waistline. If your dart take-up is less than ½" (1.3 cm), just ignore it. A dart take-up that is ½" (1.3 cm) or more will need to be sewn to give you proper fit. Skip over the ½" (1.3 cm) or more dart take-up while measuring the new waistline.

Refer to photo [D] for steps 5 and 6.

5

Refer to the instructions on the previous page to determine the difference between your pattern and your measurement. Adjust the side seam of your skirt to eliminate the extra length and ease. This is the side edge of your lowered waistline.

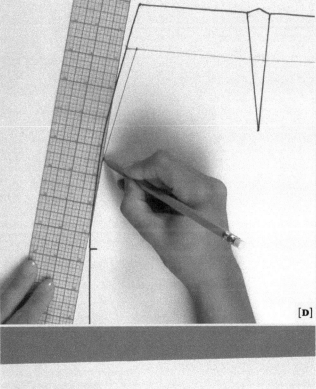

[D]

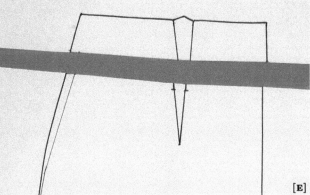

[E]

6

Draw a new side shape from the lowered waist, blending back to your master pattern's side shape at the hip level guideline.

7

Repeat these steps for the back.

8

Cut away and discard the pattern above the new lowered waistline [E].

9

Continue to draft a waistline finish. Then proceed to the skirt silhouette and/or styleline changes.

Raised Waistline

The waistline can be raised as little as ½" (1.3 cm) above the original waist or as much as the bottom of the bust. The bust creates a natural limitation to how high your raised waistline becomes; otherwise, you are designing a dress!

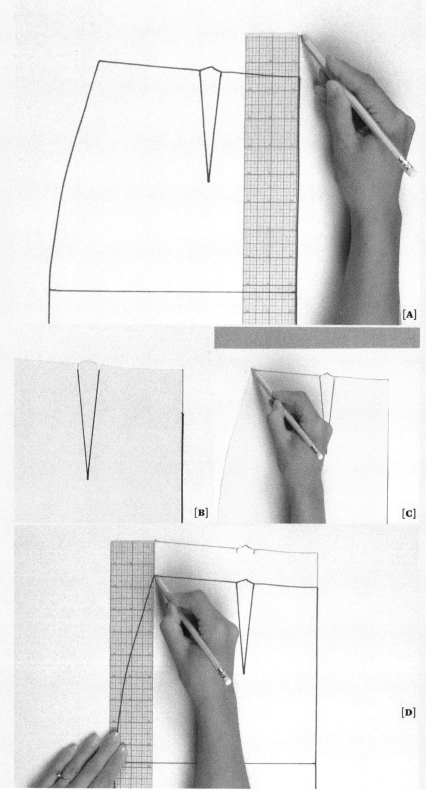

[A]

[B]

[C]

[D]

1
Trace your front skirt master pattern onto drafting paper.

2
Draw in your dart legs and hip-level guideline.

3
Raise the center front line up the amount desired for the raised waistline skirt [A].

4
Position your master pattern so that the top is at your new waistline position [B]. Draw the waistline only at the new position. Mark your dart leg positions and indicate where the side seam is [C].

5
Connect the raised waistline to the original waistline in a straight line at the side seam. This line is parallel to the center front [D].

6
Refer to the instructions on page 20 to make an adjustment to the dart take-up of your raised waistline. Divide the adjustment in half and move each dart leg by this amount. If your raised waistline is bigger than your waist, move the dart legs toward each other. Make the dart take-up smaller on the raised waistline than the original waistline [E].

If your raised waistline is smaller than your waist, move the dart legs away from each other. Make the raised waistline dart wider than the original waistline [G].

If your raised waist is the same as your original waist, keep the dart take-up the same.

7
Connect the dart position on the raised waistline to the dart position on the original waistline [F],[G].

8
Trace your back skirt master pattern onto drafting paper.

TIP

A facing works nicely with a raised waistline, helping support the extra height. Draft your facing from the raised waistline to at least 1" (2.5 cm) below the original waistline. See page 26 for instructions.

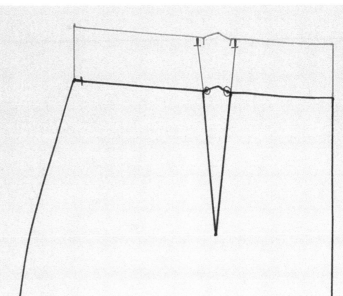

[G]

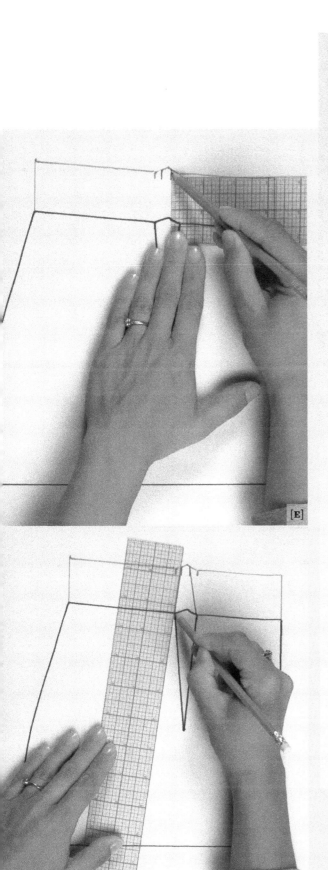

[E]

[F]

9
Draw in your dart legs and hip-level guideline.

10
Raise the center back line up the amount desired for the raised waistline skirt. Make sure this line is perpendicular to the hip-level guideline [H].

11
Follow steps 4–7 for the back.

12
Notch the darts on the raised waistline, the original waistline at the side seam, and the hip-level guideline on the side seam. Awl punch ⅛" (3 mm) inside the dart legs on the original waistline.

13
Continue to draft a waistline finish. Then proceed to the skirt silhouette and/or styleline changes.

[H]

Waistline Finishes

Once you have designed your waistline height, it is time to select how you want to finish it. There are several finish options to choose from, including a straight waistband; a facing; a contoured waistband; or a yoke—the latter three designs are all created using the same principles.

A facing cannot be seen on the outside of the finished garment; it is only apparent on the inside. A contoured waistband and yoke are both visibly seamed on the outside of the garment. The contoured waistband may or may not allow for the removal of the darts and will have an extension, as the zipper does not pass through the waistband. A yoke typically removes all the darts and a zipper passes through it to the waistline. All three of these finishes work well on waistlines of all heights—natural, raised, or lowered—though with a raised waistline the darts will still be present in the waistline finish.

Each finish has its own look and feel. Choose your finish based on what is flattering and comfortable for your body and marries nicely with your design.

Straight Waistband

A straight waistband will sit best if it is at your natural waistline, essentially sewn on top of your skirt master pattern's waistline. The best finished waistband height is between ¾ and 2 inches (1.8 and 5.1 cm). This waistband style is not a good choice for a lowered waistline. Typically, a straight waistband is folded at the top edge and the raw edges are sewn to the skirt's waistline.

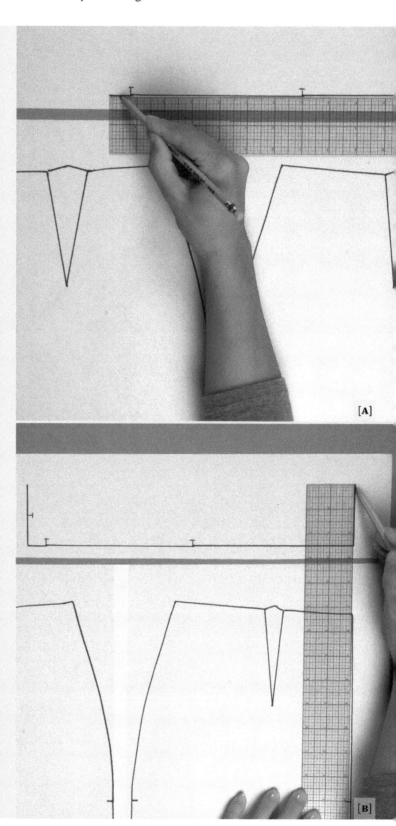

[A]

[B]

You have a choice of grainlines on a straight waistband: straight, cross, or bias. A straight grainline is the most efficient use of your fabric and will be stable. The cross grain will be the least forgiving but the most stable choice. If you cut the waistband on the cross grain, be sure to pretreat your fabric first, to eliminate shrinkage. A bias grainline will be the most forgiving and the least efficient use of your fabric. The bias grainline is great for getting a bit of contouring out of a straight waistband and can be a fun design decision depending on your fabric choice.

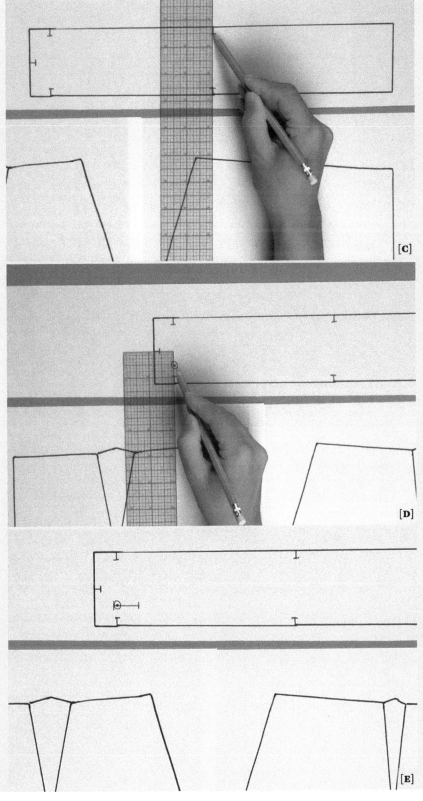

[C]

[D]

[E]

1
Measure your front master pattern waistline, not including dart take-up, and note this measurement. Do the same for the back.

Refer to photo [A] for steps 2–4.

2
Draw a horizontal line the length of the front waist measurement and notch to mark the placement of the side seam.

3
Continue to add the length of the back measurement to the line, and notch to indicate the placement of the center back.

4
Again, continue to add length to the line for a closure extension, usually the diameter of your button, snap, or hook and bar closure.

5
On both sides, draw a line perpendicular to the waist-line double the desired height of the waistband, ¾" to 2" (1.8 to 5.1 cm). Notch the midline to indicate the top folded edge of the finished waistband [B].

6
Transfer the notches to the other side of the waistband to indicate the side seam and center back [C].

7
Place the button or snap on the center back guideline halfway up the finished height of the waistband [D].

8
Place a horizontal buttonhole on the waistband. Measure ⅛" (3 mm) from the center back toward the closure extension. Next, from the center back toward the side seam notch, draw a line the width of the button [E].

9
Mark your chosen grainline. Label the waistband "Cut 1 on fold of self fabric" and "Cut 1 interfacing." The interfacing should be cut on the same grainline as the self.

10
Continue to draft the skirt silhouette and/or styleline changes.

> **TIP**
>
> *Adjust the pattern for a side closure. The pattern is the full front waist measurement, notch, full back waist measurement, notch, and closure extensions on both sides. Notch the center front and center back, which will help in sewing. This cannot be cut on the fold because the front and back waist measurements are not the same length.*

Facing

A facing is the most discreet way to finish off a waistline because no part of it shows on the outside of the garment. It works on any waistline—raised, natural, or lowered. It is a great way to finish off a garment with a print or pattern that you do not want to disrupt with a waistband or yoke. A facing should always be interfaced.

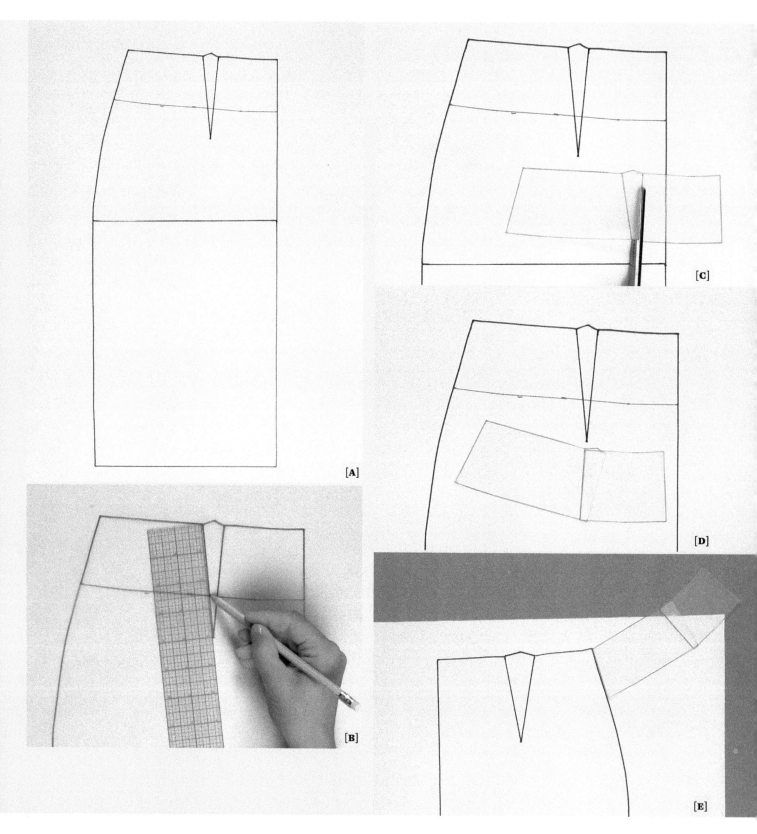

[A]

[B]

[C]

[D]

[E]

1

Trace your front skirt master pattern onto drafting paper.

2

Change your waistline, if desired.

3

Decide on the depth of your facing from the waistline, between 2" (5.1 cm) long to the base of the dart point. Draw a line down from the waist at this depth and follow the curve of the waistline to connect to the side seam [**A**].

4

On a new sheet of paper, trace the center, the waistline, and the side and bottom facing, including the dart legs [**B**].

5

On the traced copy, cut one leg of the dart and tape it on top of the uncut dart [**C**],[**D**].

6

Repeat steps 1–5 for the back skirt master pattern. Make the depth of the facing the same on the back as on the front. Use your front facing as a guide to make a smooth transition [**E**].

7

Mark your grainline parallel to the center front and center back. Cut your facing out of self fabric and interfacing and use the same cutting instructions as your front and back skirt patterns.

TIP
- -

Add a lining below a facing. Instead of tracing only the shape of the facing, trace the whole skirt. Cut the facing away, and the lower portion becomes your lining foundation. See Linings on page 172 for instructions.

Contoured Waistband

A contoured waistband is very flattering and more comfortable than a straight waistband. It is a great choice for a lowered waistline garment. It is not as efficient use of fabric as a straight waistband. A contoured waistband is typically ¾ to 3 inches (1.8 to 7.6 cm) tall.

It will have an extension at the center back to allow for a button, snap, or hook and bar closure. Unlike the straight waistband, the contoured waistband is a subtractive pattern piece: It gets cut away from your skirt pattern, as opposed to adding it on top.

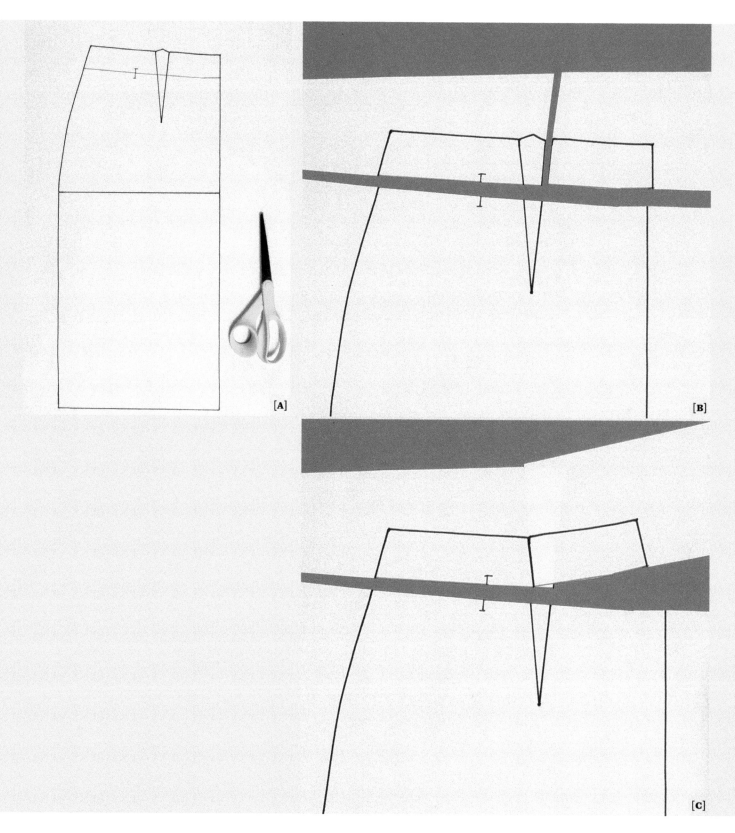

[A]

[B]

[C]

*Refer to photo [**A**] for steps 1 and 2.*

1
Follow steps 1–3 for drafting a facing (see page 26), adjusting the height of the waistband as desired.

2
Label the center front of the waistband. Place a notch across the seam of the waistline and skirt.

3
Cut the waistband away from the skirt pattern [**B**].

4
Cut one leg of the dart and tape it onto the uncut leg [**C**]. Fill as much as ⅛" (3 mm) on the top of the waistband if there is a bit of an angle. Shave as much as ⅛" (3 mm) from the bottom of the waistband if there is a sharp bend [**D**].

5
Trace your back skirt master pattern onto drafting paper. If a front waistline adjustment was made, do the same for the back.

6
Tape your waistband front to the side seam of the skirt back, matching up the waistline. Connect the side waistband depth to the center back, following the curve of your original waistline. Place a notch at the side seam [**E**].

TIP

- -

If your contoured waistband is super curvy, separate the front and back pattern pieces at the side seam. Place the grainlines parallel to the center front and back. Change your cutting instructions for the front to "Cut 2 on fold of self fabric" and the back to "Cut 4 of self fabric." Interface at least one side of the waistband. This pattern adjustment creates a side seam in your waistband while saving you a bit of fabric.

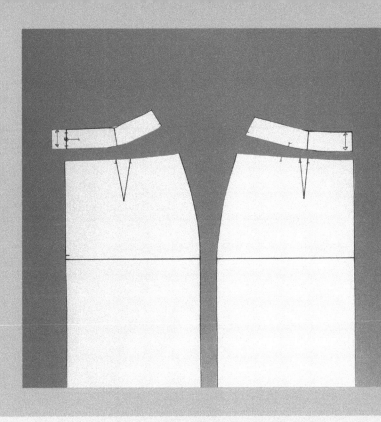

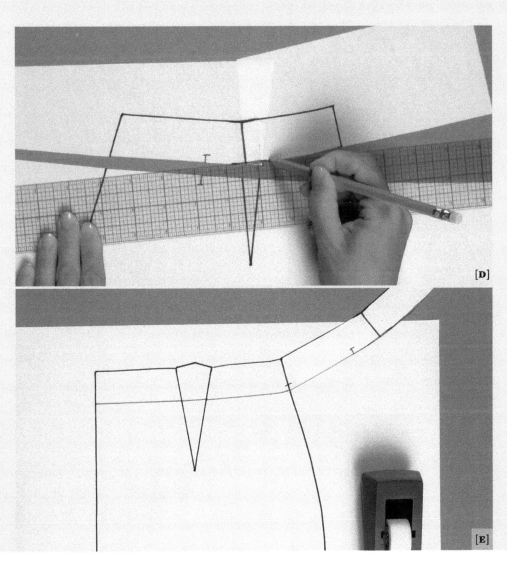

[D]

[E]

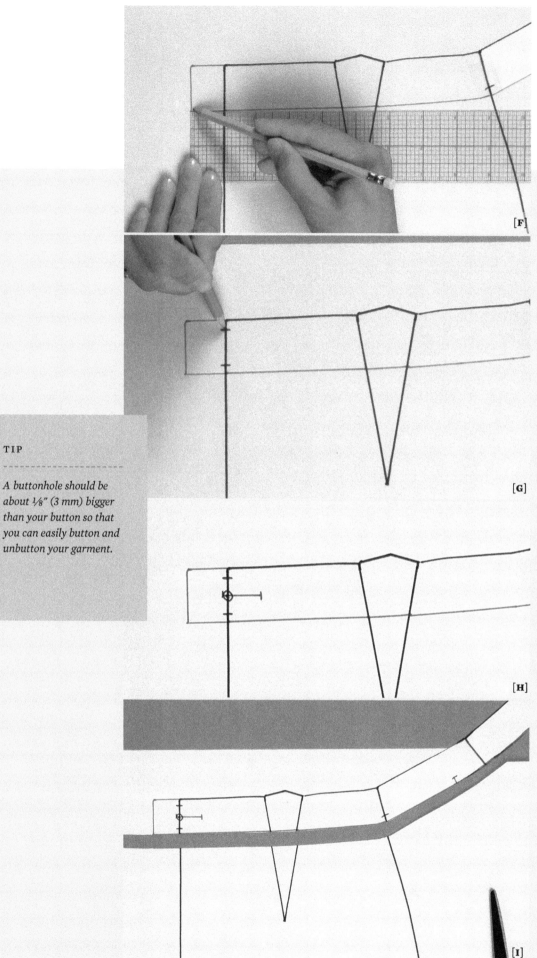

[F]

[G]

[H]

[I]

7

Extend the waistband at the center back for a closure extension, typically the diameter of the button, snap, or hook and bar closure. Place notches at the top and bottom of the waistband at center back [F]. Place notches at the top and bottom of the waistband in the center back [G].

Refer to photo [H] for steps 8 and 9.

8

On the waistband, place the button or snap on the center back guideline halfway up the finished height of the waistband.

9

Place a horizontal buttonhole on the waistband. Measure ⅛" (3 mm) from the center back toward the closure extension. Then, from the center back toward the side seam notch, draw a line the width of the button.

10

Cut the back waistband from the back skirt [I].

TIP

A buttonhole should be about ⅛" (3 mm) bigger than your button so that you can easily button and unbutton your garment.

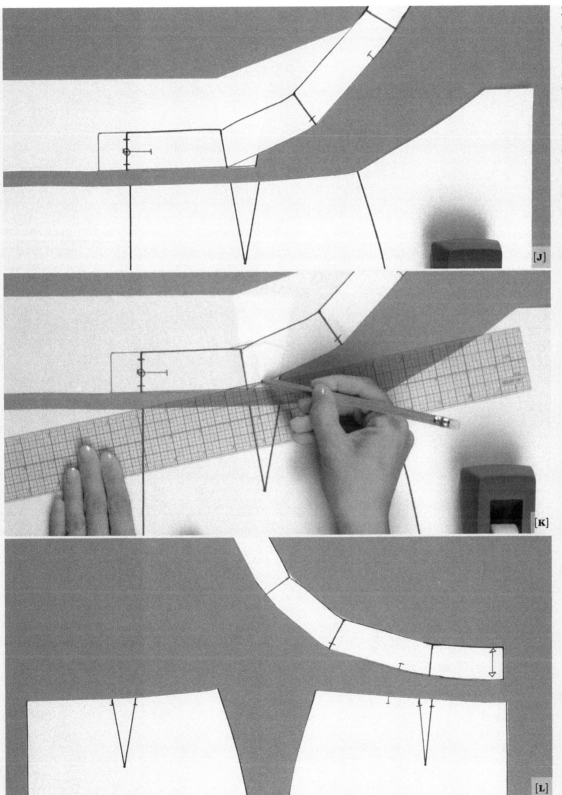

11
Cut one leg of the dart and tape it onto the uncut leg [J]. Fill as much as ⅛" (3 mm) on the top of the waistband if there is a bit of an angle. Shave as much as ⅛" (3 mm) from the bottom of the waistband if there is a sharp bend [K].

12
Place the grainline parallel to the center front. Label the waistband "Cut 2 on fold of self fabric" and "Cut 1 or 2 on fold of interfacing," depending on the fabric choice and desired structure.

13
Mark any darts that remain in the body of the skirt that need to be sewn. If they are ¼" (6 mm) or less, shave the dart take-up off of the side seam and blend to the hip-level guideline [L].

14
Continue to make changes to the silhouette and/or stylelines of your skirt.

[J]

[K]

[L]

Yoke

A yoke looks very much like a contoured waistband. Yokes are typically wider than a waistband, and the styleline at the base of the yoke is not always parallel to the waistline. A yoke has a zipper run through it unlike a waistband.

The yoke can create interesting stylelines that take all of the dart shaping out, creating a more contoured pattern piece.

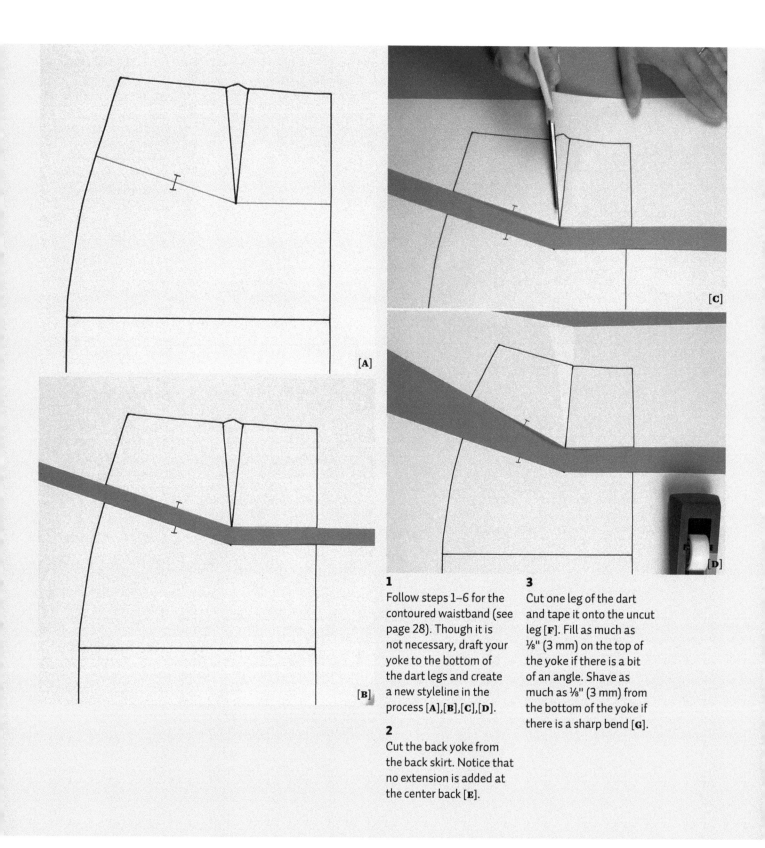

[A]

[B]

[C]

[D]

1

Follow steps 1–6 for the contoured waistband (see page 28). Though it is not necessary, draft your yoke to the bottom of the dart legs and create a new styleline in the process [A],[B],[C],[D].

2

Cut the back yoke from the back skirt. Notice that no extension is added at the center back [E].

3

Cut one leg of the dart and tape it onto the uncut leg [F]. Fill as much as ⅛" (3 mm) on the top of the yoke if there is a bit of an angle. Shave as much as ⅛" (3 mm) from the bottom of the yoke if there is a sharp bend [G].

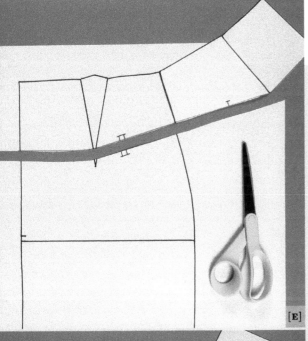

[E]

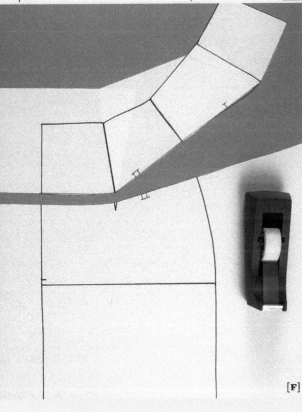

[F]

4
Place the grainline parallel to the center front. Label the yoke "Cut 2 on fold of self fabric" and "Cut 1 or 2 on fold of interfacing," depending on the fabric choice and desired structure [H].

5
Mark any darts that remain in the body of the skirt that need to be sewn. If they are ¼" (6 mm) or less, shave the dart take-up off of the side seam and blend to the hip-level guideline.

6
Continue to make changes to the silhouette and/or stylelines of your skirt.

TIP

Create a dramatic style-line across the yoke and still take the shaping of the darts away.

[H]

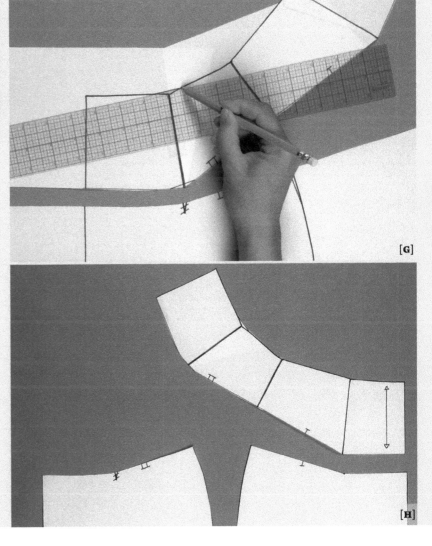

[G]

[H]

Flare

There are several types of flare skirts, from a simple A-line to a full circle and everything in between. The type of fabric you select and the grainline you cut it on will result in very different effects.

The common thread with flared skirts is that they are fitted at the waist with all the fullness at the hem, making them different from a gathered or pleated skirt, which has added fullness at the waistline.

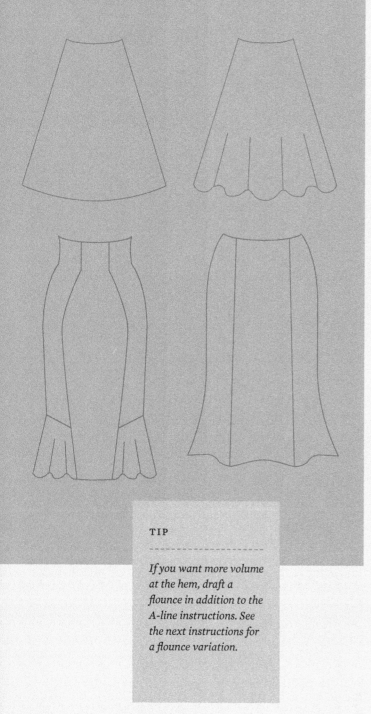

TIP

- - - - - - - - - - - - - - - - - - - -

If you want more volume at the hem, draft a flounce in addition to the A-line instructions. See the next instructions for a flounce variation.

A-Line Flare

An A-line flare is a structured bell-shaped skirt. It fits close to the body from waist to hip with the fullness below the hip to the hem. Combine the A-line instructions with the Flounce instructions on page 36 to design a skirt with more volume at the hem that you can twirl in.

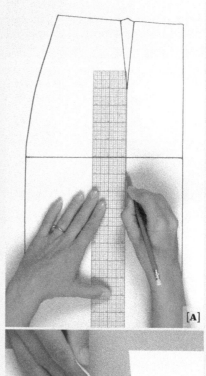

[A]

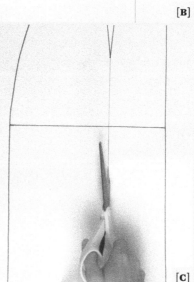

[B]

[C]

1
Trace your front skirt master pattern. Make any changes to the waistline and waist finish.

2
Draw a line perpendicular to the hip-level guideline from the dart point to the skirt hem. This is your insertion line [A].

3
Cut one leg of the dart (it does not matter which leg) from the waist to the point of the dart but not through it [B].

4
Cut the insertion line from the hem to the point of the dart, not through it. The paper should be tethered at your dart point, allowing you to pivot your work around. If your paper becomes separated, your dart point is the pivot point [C].

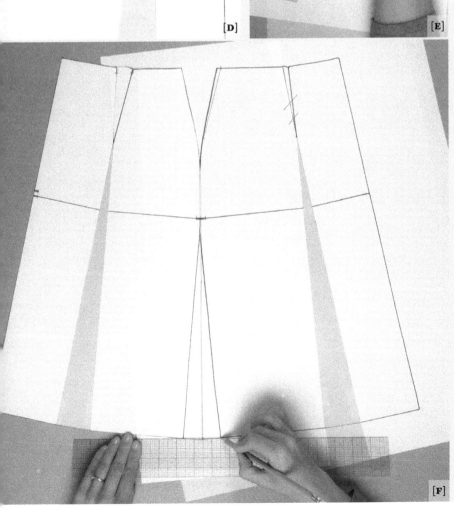

[D]

[E]

[F]

Refer to photo [D] for steps 5 and 6.

5
Place additional paper underneath the skirt pattern.

6
Close the dart by moving the cut dart leg to the uncut dart leg, overlapping the dart take-up. This opens the hem of the skirt, creating flare or volume. Add the most volume by closing the entire dart; for a little volume, leave some dart take-up remaining.

7
Tape in position. Connect the hem across the insertion. Smooth out any points by slightly curving the line if necessary.

8
At the side seam, extend the hem half the amount you inserted. For example, if you inserted 2" (5.1 cm), add 1" (2.5 cm) at the side. Connect the extension at the base to, or slightly above, the hip-level guideline to create a straight shape at the side. To achieve a straighter side shape, you can cut off as much as was added in the insertion on the hip-level guideline [E].

Refer to photo [F] for steps 9–11.

9
If ⅜" (1 cm) or more dart take-up remains at your waistline, mark its new legs with notches. If less than ⅜" (1 cm) dart take-up remains, shave the dart take-up off the side seam from the waist, blending down the length of the dart.

10
Add the same volume to the skirt back insertion and extension as the skirt front. For example, if your front has a 2" (5.1 cm) insertion, insert 2" (5.1 cm) to the back as well.

11
Place your front and back skirt patterns together at the side seams and smooth out any points at the hem.

12
Mark your grainline parallel to the center front and center back. Label your front skirt "Cut 1 on fold of self fabric" and the back "Cut 2 of self fabric."

> **TIP**
>
> *Change your grainline from length to bias for a skirt with a softer drape that hugs the hips a little. Use a fabric with a softer hand and a nice drape.*

> **TIP**
>
> *The A-line flare can have a curved hem, making it difficult to fold the hem under. Draft a hem facing, following the instructions on page 167.*

Flounce Variation

The flounce is a great technique if you want volume in a specific area. There are endless possibilities where you can use this technique. This technique is being shown on a styleline, but it can just as easily be done at the waistline.

> **TIP**
> ---------------------
> *Trace the full skirt front by copying both the right and left side and drafting a flounce on an asymmetric styleline.*

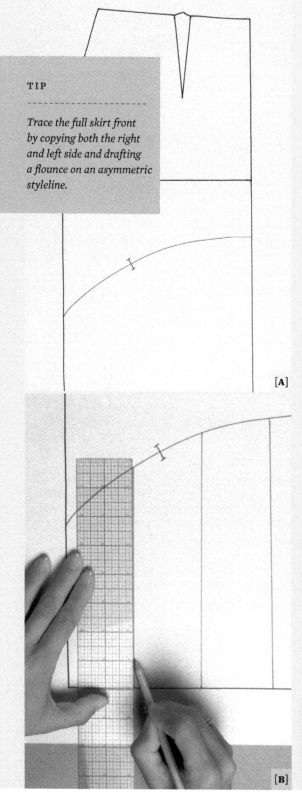

[A]

[B]

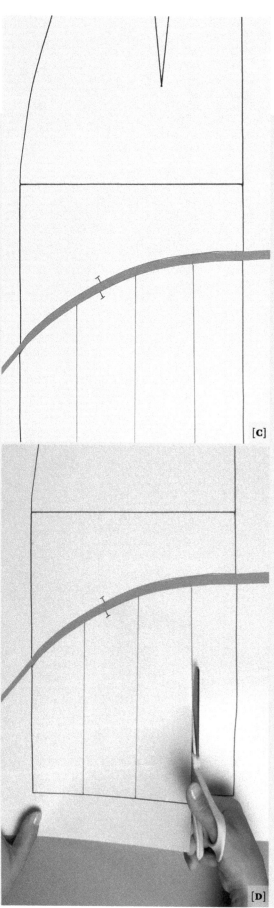

[C]

[D]

1

Trace your skirt master pattern. Make any changes to the waistline and waist finish.

2

Draw in the desired styleline. Mark notches across the styleline [A].

3

Draw in as few or as many insertion lines parallel to the center [B].

4

Cut the skirt apart on the drawn styleline [C].

5

Cut the insertion lines from the hem to, but not through, the styleline. To keep your work manageable, cut the insertion lines one at a time [D].

6

Place additional paper behind the flounce and insert as little or as much volume into the flounce as desired [E]. Secure it in place with tape. Do not allow your pattern piece to overlap itself, making it impossible to add seam allowance [F].

7
Connect the hem across the insertion points and thoroughly smooth any points to create a soft curve [**G**].

8
The grainline can be parallel or bias to the center. Wherever the straight of grain falls on the cut fabric will be more stable and have less hem flutter or drape. Your cutting instructions will vary depending on what you have designed. In general, they will be the same as the front and back of the skirt [**H**].

[**H**]

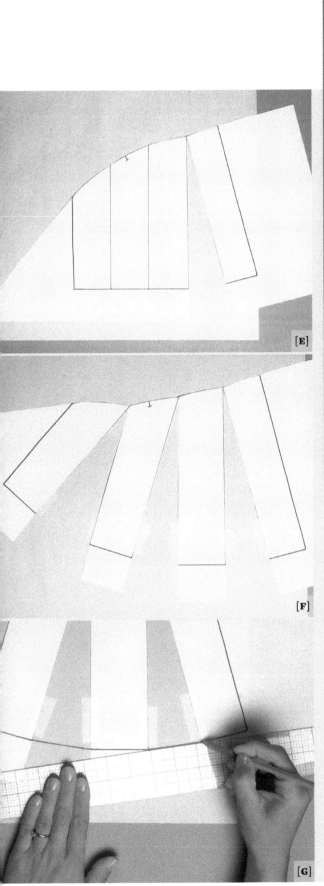

[**E**]

[**F**]

[**G**]

VARIATIONS

Create a full or partial circle skirt by drafting a flounce from the waistline.

—

Add a flounce on a flounce.

—

Vary the amount of volume added at each insertion.

Flare Extension

Flare can also be added to vertical stylelines to create seams that flare out. This method is not appropriate for side seams alone. When combined with the stylelines pattern (see page 40), more volume can be added to the side seams. Read ahead to draft a vertical styleline and add flare to it.

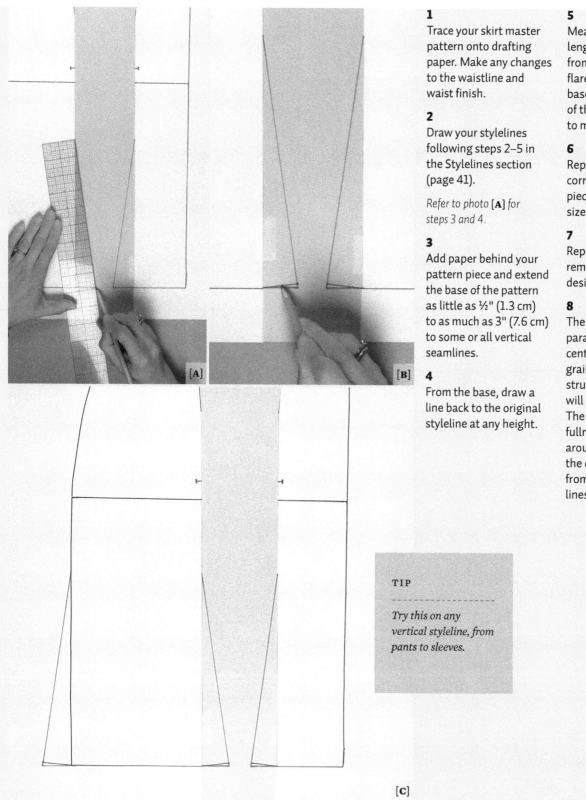

[A]

[B]

[C]

1
Trace your skirt master pattern onto drafting paper. Make any changes to the waistline and waist finish.

2
Draw your stylelines following steps 2–5 in the Stylelines section (page 41).

Refer to photo [A] for steps 3 and 4.

3
Add paper behind your pattern piece and extend the base of the pattern as little as ½" (1.3 cm) to as much as 3" (7.6 cm) to some or all vertical seamlines.

4
From the base, draw a line back to the original styleline at any height.

5
Measure the original length of the styleline from the height of the flare extensions to the base. Adjust the base of the flared styleline to match [B].

6
Repeat steps 3–5 for the corresponding pattern piece, adding the same size extension.

7
Repeat steps 3–6 for all remaining stylelines as desired [C].

8
The grainline can be parallel or bias to the center. The straight of grain will be more structured and seams will really hold the flare. The bias will add soft fullness all the way around the base. Follow the cutting instructions from step 6 of the Stylelines section, page 41.

> **TIP**
>
> *Try this on any vertical styleline, from pants to sleeves.*

Pencil

A pencil silhouette is very simple to draft. It creates a pegged hemline. How much you peg or taper your hemline is dependent on the length of your skirt and your ability to walk!

Measure the new base front and back, and then multiply by 2. Wrap a tape measure to that measurement and hold it around your legs at the hem length and see how it feels.

1
Trace your front and back skirt master pattern. Make any changes to the waistline and waist finish.

2
Decide the amount to taper the hem, ranging from ½" to 1½" (1.3 to 3.8 cm).

The amount you choose to taper will vary depending on your skirt's length and your figure [A].

3
Mark the same taper amount in from your side seam at the base on the front and back.

4
Connect the base to the 2" (5.1 cm) below your hip level guideline on the side seam, creating a new side shape. Continue to add stylelines if desired [B].

5
Draw grainline parallel to the center front and back. Label the front skirt pattern "Cut 1 on fold of self fabric" and the back "Cut 2 of self fabric."

[A]

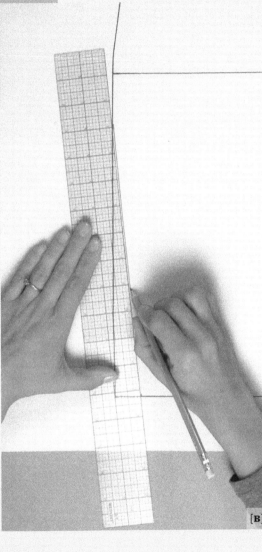

[B]

TIPS

Add slits, vents, or pleats to any seam and allow for more mobility in a very pegged skirt. See page 168 for instructions.

See Hem Finishes on page 166 for instructions on how to draft a hem for a skirt with a tapered base.

Stylelines

There are endless variations of stylelines. They can be used for shaping in place of darts so they can really shape around the contours of your body. They can be symmetrical or asymmetrical, and so much more.

Drawing a Styleline

In addition to serving an aesthetic purpose, a styleline can be a more accurate way to conform to your body's shape than using a dart, especially in a fitted skirt.

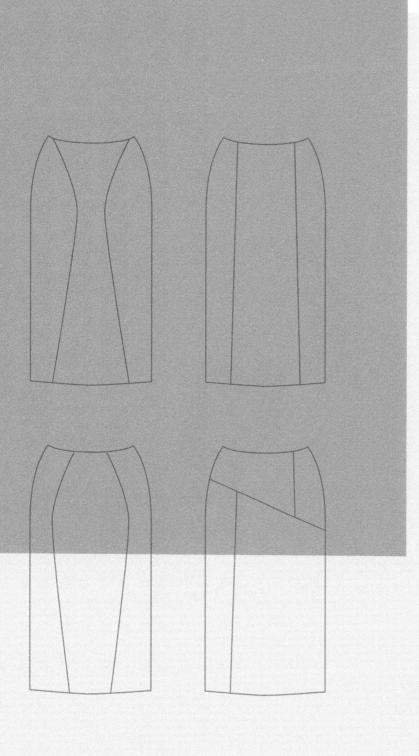

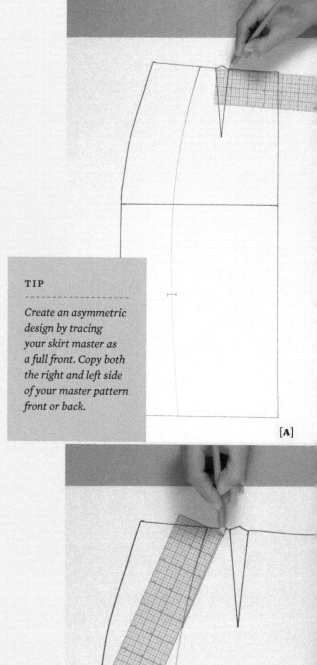

TIP

Create an asymmetric design by tracing your skirt master as a full front. Copy both the right and left side of your master pattern front or back.

[A]

[B]

1
Trace your skirt master pattern. Make any changes to the waistline and waist finish.

2
Draw in your desired stylelines. Mark notches across the styleline, making sure their position is unique, so that they are helpful when sewing. Your stylelines do not need to pass directly through the darts, but the closer they are to the original dart position, the better the fit will be [**A**].

3
Measure your dart take-up to one side of the new styleline. Draw a new dart leg to one side of the styleline [**B**]. An adjustment to the dart leg length may need to be made; do this at the waistline [**C**].

4
Draw your grainline parallel to the center front and on each pattern piece.

5
Cut your pattern pieces apart along the styleline and discard the dart take-up [**D**].

6
Cutting information will vary depending on where you choose to place your stylelines. The examples shown are as follows. Label the center front "Cut 1 on fold of self fabric." Label the center back, side back, and side front "Cut 2 of self fabric."

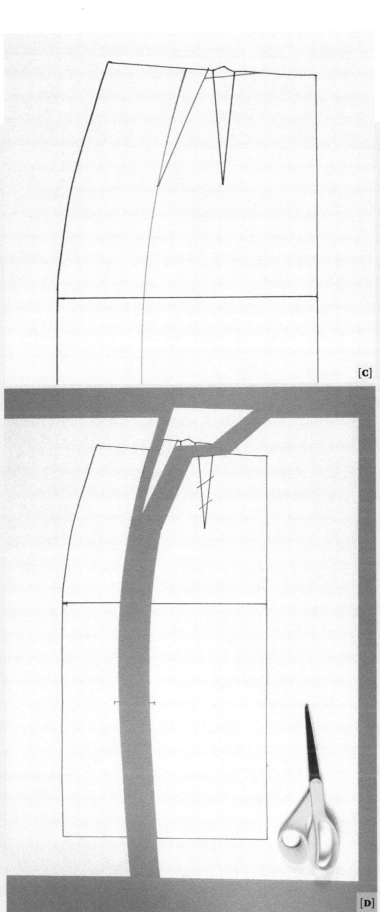

[**C**]

[**D**]

TIP

Flare the seamlines. See Flare Extension on page 38.
—OR—
Try pegging the base on the styleline using the same method as the pencil silhouette.

Gathers

One might think of a gathered skirt simply as a rectangle sewn into a waistband. I encourage you to give them more credit.

Gathered skirts can be very full and gathered around the entire waist, or you can choose to just gather small sections of your skirt, creating light or full volume in very specific places.

Depending on the fabric you choose, the gathering can add dramatically different amounts of volume. As you did in the flare exercise, you will be creating insertion lines, only this time you will add volume at the waist. Typically, the dart is absorbed into the gathers and can mostly be ignored.

TIPS

See how gathering creates volume in a specific fabric by testing it and adjust your patterns insertions accordingly.

Combine the gathers with a flare technique for a hem with a larger sweep.

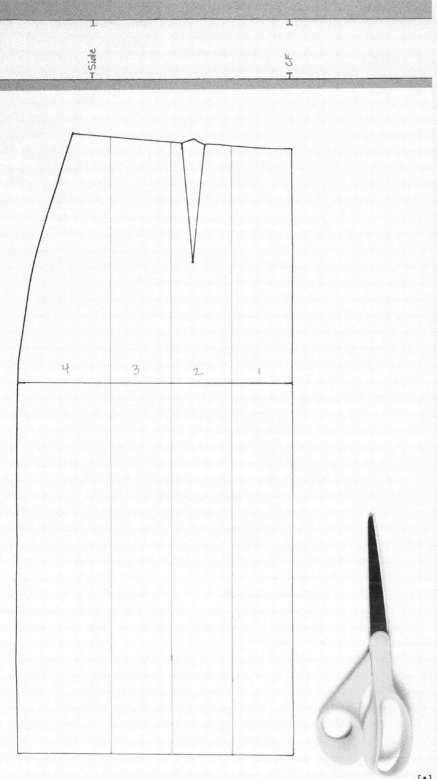

1
Trace your front skirt master pattern onto drafting paper. Make any changes to the waistline and waist finish.

Refer to photo [A] for steps 2–4.

2
Decide where you want to place your insertion lines. If you want a fully gathered skirt, you can position multiple insertion lines on the front and back. If gathering only in small sections of the skirt is desired, place one or a few insertion lines in a specific area.

3
Place notches to each side of the insertion line; the spacing can be anywhere from ½" to 2" (1.3 to 5.1 cm) to each side of the insertion line. Measure and note the space between notches before making insertions. This is the space the gathers will be sewn to. Gathering takes up more space in a heavyweight fabric than in a lighter weight fabric. If you are gathering a skirt to a styleline or waistband, you can place the notches across the styleline or waistband.

4
Number your sections across the insertion lines so that you can put it back together in the correct order.

TIP

If you plan to gather near your dart take-up, just ignore the dart.

[A]

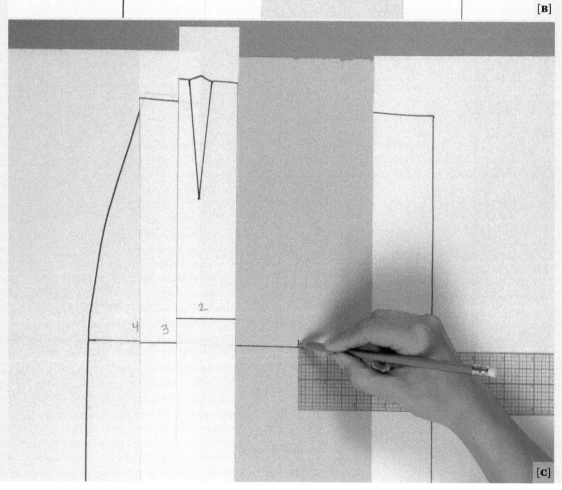

TIPS

If you have inserted more than 3" (7.6 cm) of volume in any given insertion, straighten out your side seams during the fitting to remove some of the side curve.

Insertion amounts can vary; use more notches to indicate a different distribution of gathers.

5
Cut your pattern piece on the insertion lines. To keep your work manageable, cut the insertion lines one at a time.

6
Secure paper behind the first section and extend your hip-level and hem guidelines onto the paper [**B**].

7
From the first pattern section, measure over the amount of volume desired, typically double to triple the space between notches. Less insertion is needed for a heavyweight fabric and more insertion for a lightweight fabric [**C**].

[**B**]

[**C**]

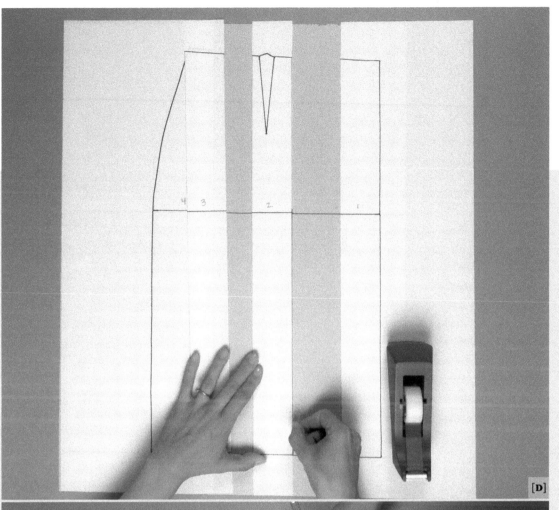

[D]

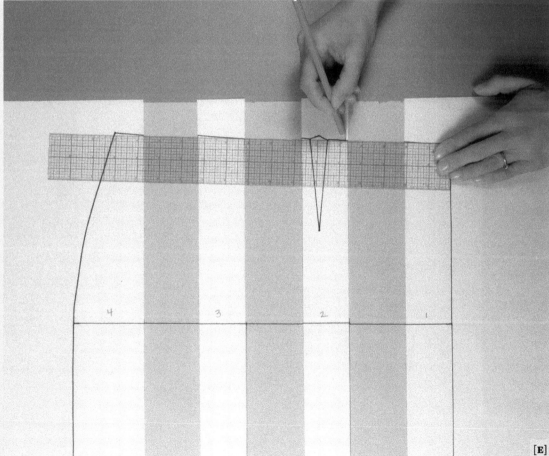

[E]

8

Align the hem and hip-level guidelines and secure the second pattern section to the paper [D].

Refer to photo [E] for steps 9 and 10.

9

Repeat steps 5–8 for all insertion lines.

10

Smooth the shape of the waistline or styleline to remove any sharp points or uneven lines.

11

Draw the grainline parallel to the center front and back. Label the front skirt pattern "Cut 1 on fold of self fabric" and the back "Cut 2 of self fabric."

TIP

- - - - - - - - - - - - - - - - - - - -

Do a reverse flair. Add volume only at the waist, not at the hem.

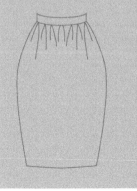

Pleats

There are several kinds of pleats and, for the most part, they are drafted the same way. If pleats are formed on stylelines or insertion lines, they will behave the best if the lines are placed on the length grain or cross grain. They become unstable and unstructured when placed off-grain.

Depending on your fabric and construction, pleats can take on many different appearances. An unpressed pleat will add soft volume that billows slightly at the hem, whereas a fabric with crisply pressed or edgestitched pleats will be much more angular and geometric in appearance. Be sure to test your fabric to find out what will work best, because your fabric will often tell you. If the fabric doesn't hold a press well, it is best not to fight it. A fabric that loves to be pressed will hold crisp pleats longer.

TIP

Pleats can be secured only at the waist or sewn down a certain depth from the waist. Mark the top of the pleats with notches and the depth the pleats are to be sewn down to with awl punches ⅛" (3 mm) inside the foldlines of your pleat.

Pleat Types

The differences in pleat types come from the way the fabric is folded and how much pleat volume is inserted into your pattern. Knife pleats are generally placed every 1 inch (2.5 cm) and all pleats are pressed in one direction.

A box pleat can be 3 inches (7.6 cm) wide with half the pleats pressed to the right and the other half to the left.

TIPS

Remember that your center front is cut on the fold, so if you are inserting many pleats equidistant to each other, the insertion line closest to the center front should be half the distance of the other pleats. Alternatively, if the pleat is on the center front you can extend paper beyond the center front guideline for the pleat.

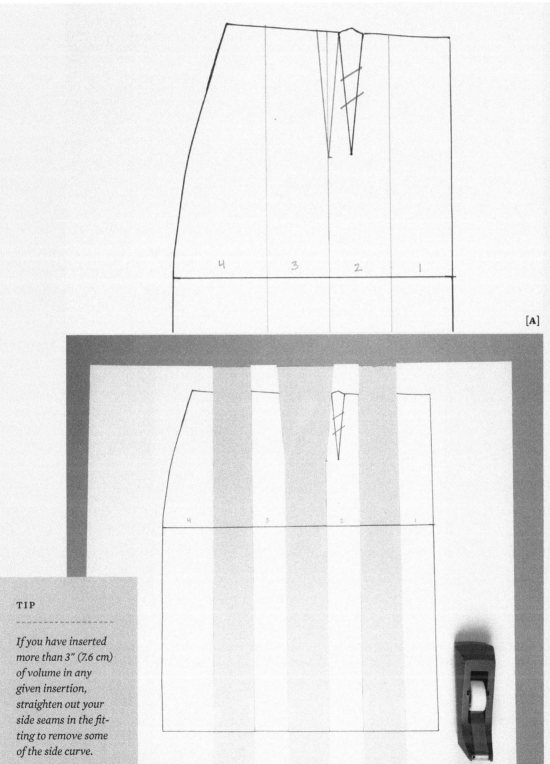

[A]

[B]

TIP

If you have inserted more than 3" (7.6 cm) of volume in any given insertion, straighten out your side seams in the fitting to remove some of the side curve.

1
Trace your front skirt master pattern onto drafting paper. Make any changes to the waistline or waist finish.

2
Decide where you want to place your pleat(s) and draw in the insertion or styleline(s) perpendicular to your hip-level guideline. If you have many pleat insertions, number them so that you can put it back together in the correct order [A].

Refer to photo [B] for steps 3–6.

3
Cut along your insertion lines. To keep your work manageable, cut the insertion lines one at a time.

4
Secure paper behind the first cut section and extend your hip-level and hem guideline onto the paper.

5
Measure over from the first pattern section double the amount of the finished width of the pleat.

For a knife pleat, insert 2" (5 cm), fold one side of the insertion line, and place the folded paper on top of the other side of the insertion line.

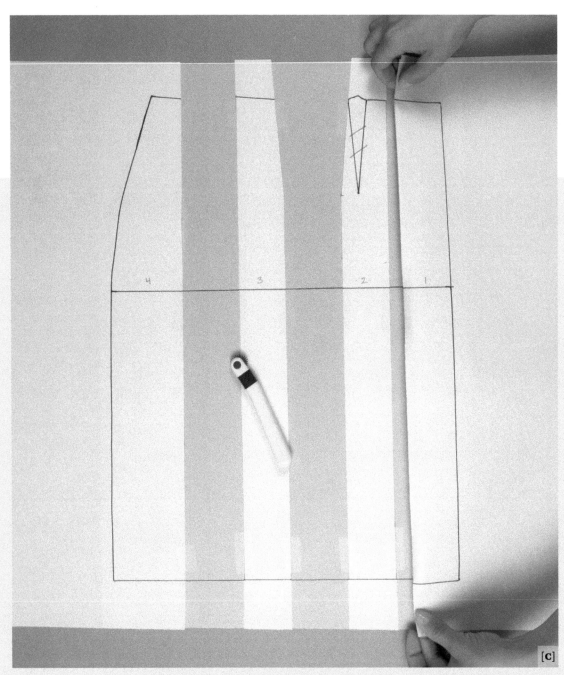

For a box pleat, insert four times the finished pleat size and fold each side of your pleat to the center of the insertion.

Adjust the insertion size if the pleat is too small or too large.

6

Align the hem and hip-level guidelines and secure a second pattern section to the paper.

7

Fold the paper the way you want your pleats folded in your sewn garment [C].

[C]

TIP

If your dart is in the way, it can be absorbed to one or both sides of the pleat. Make sure your notch includes dart take-up.

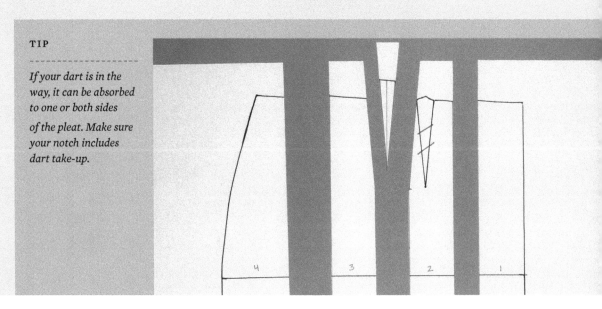

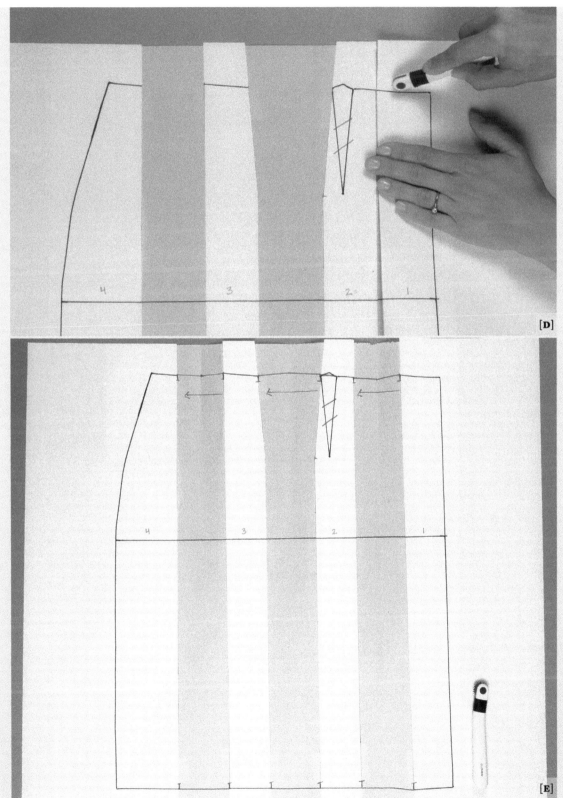

[D]

[E]

8

With a tracing wheel, trace the shape of the waistline and hem through the folded paper. Unfold and draw the traced shape [**D**].

9

Place notches on each side of the insertion line at the waistline and at the hem [**E**].

10

Repeat for all insertion lines.

11

Repeat all steps for the back, if desired.

12

Draw your grainline parallel or perpendicular to the center front and back. Label your front pattern "Cut 1 on fold of self fabric" and your back "Cut 2 of self fabric."

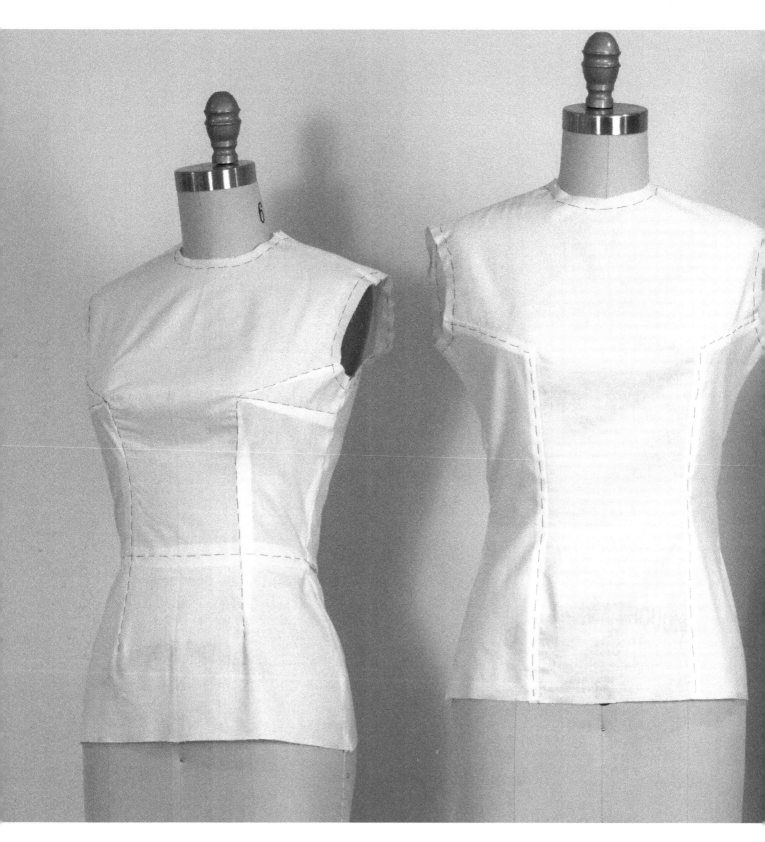

Bodice Foundation

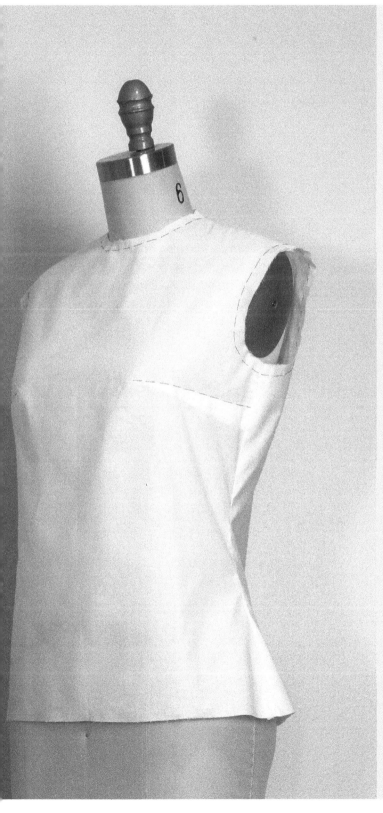

There are thousands of garment possibilities that can be designed from a bodice pattern, from crop tops to full-length gowns.

—

They generally fall into one of three categories that relate to fit and style: a bodice and skirt combination, a princess seamline conversion, and a shift or relaxed bodice.

The Master Bodice Pattern Library

Bodice Variations

From one type of master you can create any other master, but over time you may find you want your master pattern library to have one of each type in a sleeve and sleeveless version.

The bodice and skirt combination style has a waistline seam. This is the most direct adaptation of a fitting shell. This option allows for body-conscious to relaxed designs of any length.

The princess seamline conversion has vertical stylelines or princess seamlines. Making a master pattern in this style eliminates the need for a waistline seam. You can adapt your fitting shell to create a princess seamline conversion or start from a princess seamline commercial pattern. This option also allows for body-conscious to relaxed designs of any length.

The relaxed bodice will likely have side darts and may have waist darts. It lacks a waistline and vertical seams that are used for shaping. This master is not appropriate for fitted designs, but it is great for creating garments like shift dresses or button-down shirts and can be designed to any length. This can be created from a princess seamline conversion or bodice and skirt combination.

Each of these masters can be made into a sleeveless garment or one with sleeves.

Guidelines

Regardless of which bodice master you begin working with, have all your guidelines drawn on your master and know how much ease is built into the pattern on each guideline. See page 13.

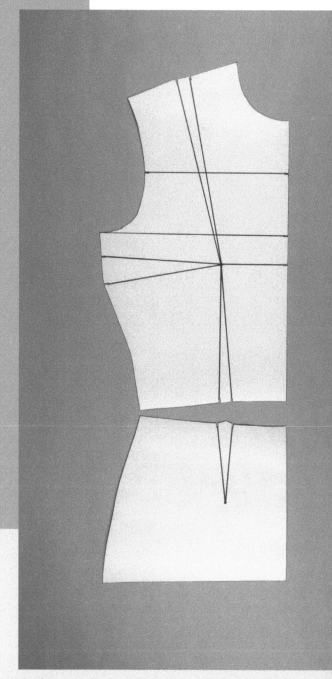

Bodice and skirt combination

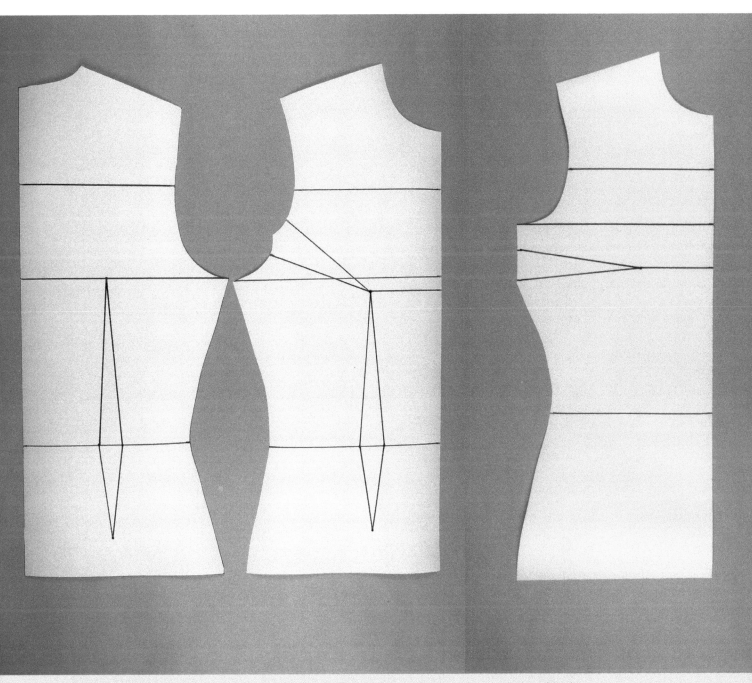

Princess seamline conversion

Relaxed bodice

Aligning the Master Bodice and Skirt Combination

On a fitting shell or other foundation pattern with a waistline seam, make sure that the waist measurement, waist dart take-up, and waist dart location match up across the waistline seam. This will make it much easier to convert this pattern to other master pattern styles as well as princess seamline and empire styleline designs.

There are two options below for aligning your bodice and skirt pattern: 1) shave off the excess dart take-up and 2) redistribute the dart take-up. Shave off the dart take-up if your bust is less full, a B cup or less, or if you prefer a silhouette that is less fitted under the bust.

Shave Off the Dart Take-Up

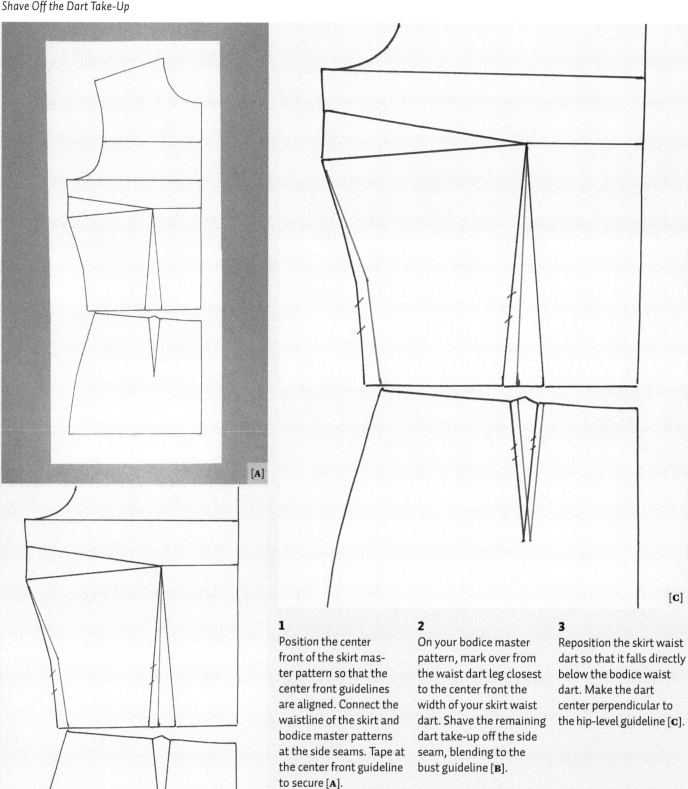

[A]

[B]

[C]

1
Position the center front of the skirt master pattern so that the center front guidelines are aligned. Connect the waistline of the skirt and bodice master patterns at the side seams. Tape at the center front guideline to secure [A].

2
On your bodice master pattern, mark over from the waist dart leg closest to the center front the width of your skirt waist dart. Shave the remaining dart take-up off the side seam, blending to the bust guideline [B].

3
Reposition the skirt waist dart so that it falls directly below the bodice waist dart. Make the dart center perpendicular to the hip-level guideline [C].

Redistribute the dart take-up if you have a fuller bust, C cup or larger, and you want shaping under the bust in your garment designs. Before beginning with either method, the waist of the bodice and skirt must be equal to each other, excluding the dart take-up. If they are not equal in measurement, choose the bodice measurement. The bodice often has more ease built in at the waistline, allowing for more comfort in a dress or blouse design.

Redistribute the Dart Take-Up

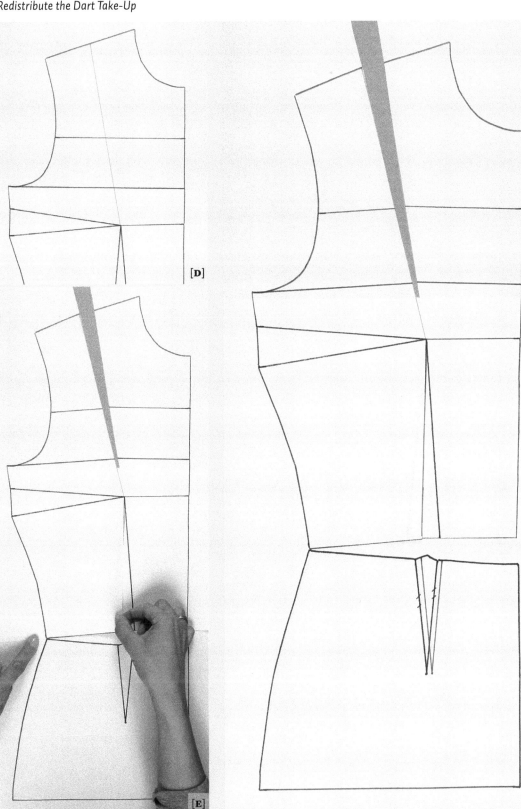

[D]

[E]

[F]

1
Position the center front of the skirt master pattern so that the center front guidelines are aligned. Connect the waistline of the skirt and bodice master patterns at the side seams. Tape at the center front guideline to secure [**A, OPPOSITE**].

2
Draw an insertion line from the center of the shoulder seam to the bust apex [**D**].

*Refer to photo [**E**] for steps 3–5.*

3
Cut the insertion line from the shoulder seam to the bust apex but not through it.

4
Cut your bodice waist dart leg closest to the side seam from the waist to the bust apex but not through it.

5
Move the cut waist dart leg toward the uncut dart leg until the bodice waist dart leg equals the size the skirt waist dart.

6
Reposition the skirt waist dart so that it falls directly below the bodice waist dart. Make the dart center perpendicular to the hip-level guideline [**F**].

Creating a Master Princess Seamline

If you already have a great jacket or dress pattern with princess seamlines but you want to have more design freedom, you can turn the pattern pieces into a master.

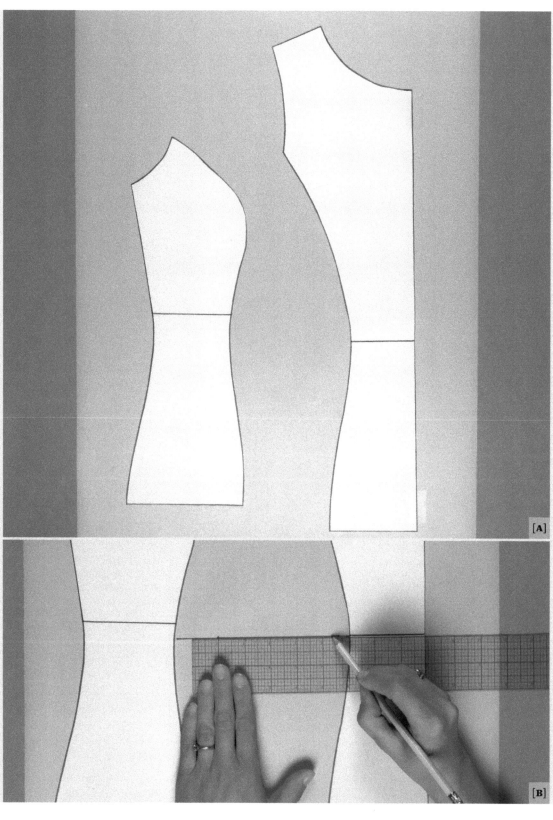

[A]

[B]

1
Trace all your princess seamline pattern pieces without seam allowance. Use the center front and not a button extension line [A].

2
Tape your center front pattern piece onto additional paper. Draw a line perpendicular to the center front guideline passing through the waist guideline on your pattern piece [B].

Refer to photo [C] for steps 3 and 4.

3
Connect the bust guideline and hip of the side front to the center front pattern pieces. Position the waist guideline of the side front pattern piece on the drawn waist guideline.

4
The pattern pieces should connect at, or very near, the bust apex. Mark this connection with an awl punch.

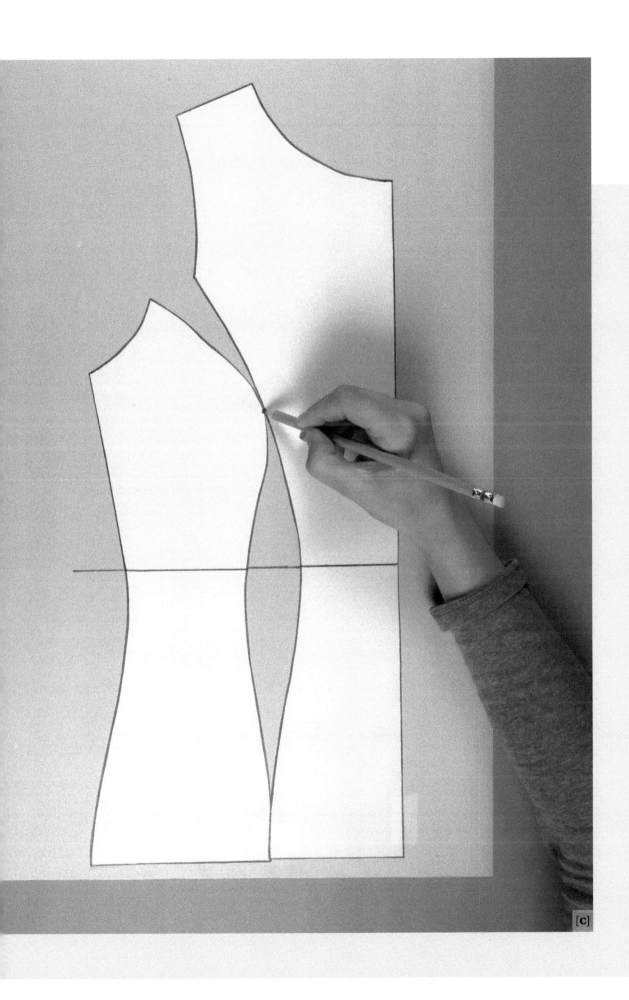

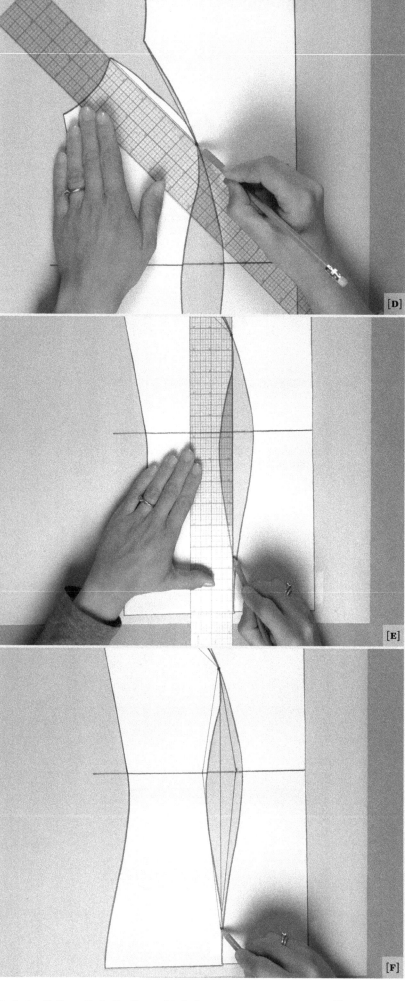

[D]

[E]

[F]

5

Simplify the seam shape to straight dart legs by connecting the gaps found between the princess seamlines to the bust apex in a straight line, whether this is from the armhole, shoulder, neck, or side seam [D].

6

Draw a line down from the bust apex perpendicular to the waist guideline to the depth where the princess seamline connects below the waist. This will be the center of a waist dart [E].

Refer to photo [F] for steps 7 and 8.

7

Measure the gap between the side front and center front princess pattern pieces. Half of this measurement goes to each side of the centerline of the dart.

8

Connect all points to draw in the waist dart.

Refer to photo [G] for steps 9 and 10.

9

Tape your center back pattern piece onto additional paper. Draw a line perpendicular to the grainline passing through the waist guideline on your pattern piece.

10

Connect the side back to the center back pattern pieces. Position the waist guideline of the side back pattern piece on the drawn waist guideline.

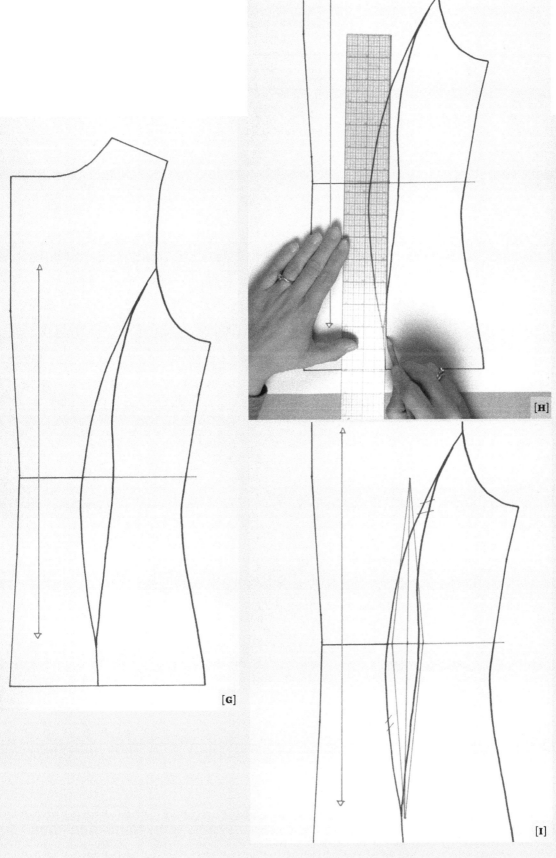

[G]

[H]

[I]

11
Measure the entire back waist from center to side, including the waist dart. Mark the center point.

12
Draw a vertical guideline perpendicular to the waist guideline passing through the center of the waist. This is the dart centerline. The top and bottom of the dart center should be level with where the side back connects to the center back on the princess seamline [**H**].

13
Measure the gap between the side back and the center back princess pattern pieces. Half of this measurement goes to each side of the centerline of the dart. Connect all points to draw in the waist dart [**I**].

14
Create a princess seamline master pattern, if desired.

Relaxed Bodice Master

Not every garment has either a waistline seam or a princess seam. Although garments drafted with these elements will provide the best fit with minimal ease, they will not create a relaxed button-down shirt or casual shift dress. This is yet another master pattern that can be created. In a garment that is relatively relaxed, especially at the waist, the waist darts can often be ignored. These drafting instructions will allow you to design garments that lack princess and waistline seams.

When using a princess seamline conversion, simply ignore the front and/or back waist darts and add extra ease at the side seam, if desired. Otherwise, use your aligned bodice and skirt master patterns and follow the instructions below.

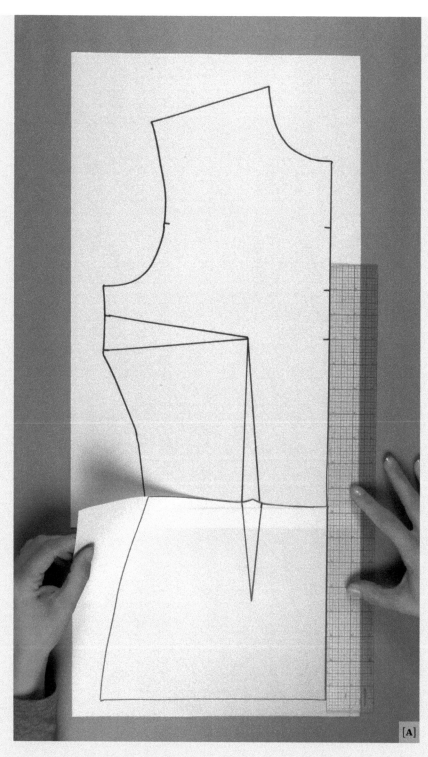

[A]

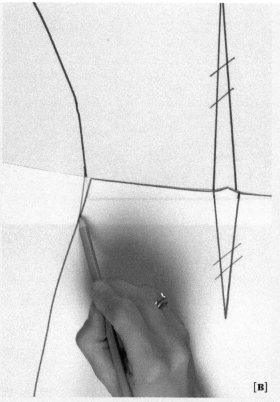

[B]

Refer to photo [A] for steps 1–3.

1
Draw your bodice master onto drafting paper, making sure you leave extra paper below, as long as the garment length is desired. Be sure to have made adjustments to the waist dart of the bodice and skirt so that their dart take-up is the same. See instructions on page 54 for Aligning the Master Bodice and Skirt Combination.

2
Draw a continuation of the center front guideline below the waistline.

3
Place the skirt master pattern on the extended center front guideline so that the waist of the skirt connects with the waist of the bodice. There is often overlap at the side seam.

4
Smooth out any dips at the waistline as little as ⅛" (3 mm). For more ease, connect the bust guideline to the hip-level guideline in a straight line [B].

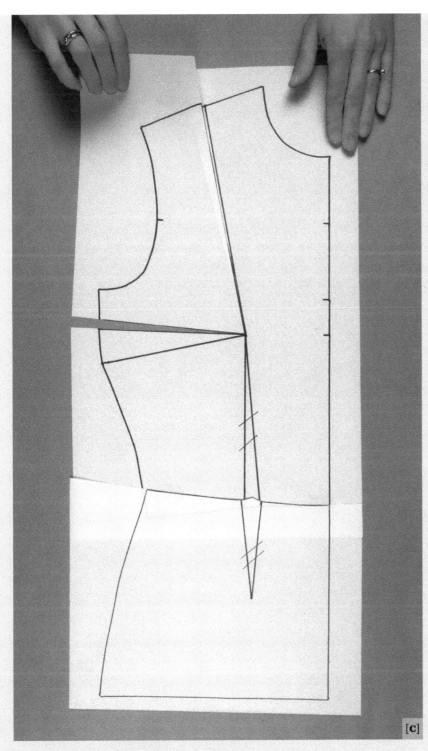

[C]

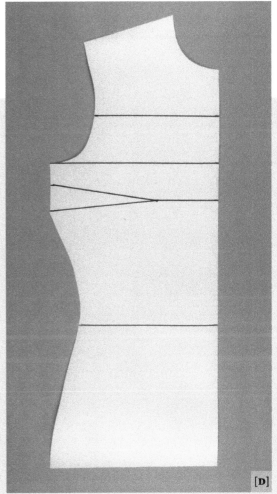

[D]

Refer to photo [C] for steps 5 and 6.

5

If you are using the aligned bodice and skirt master pattern that has a shoulder dart, cut one leg of the shoulder dart from the shoulder seam to the bust apex but not through it. Cut one leg of the side dart from the side seam to the bust apex but not through it.

6

Take the cut leg of the shoulder dart and place it on top of the uncut leg. The side dart will become larger.

7

Repeat steps 1–4 for the back.

8

Create a relaxed bodice master, if desired.

TIP

- - - - - - - - - - - - - - -

This master can create a great pattern for a shift dress or relaxed blouse by ignoring all, or part of, the waist dart.

Lengthening or Shortening Your Bodice Master Pattern

Designs of any length can be created from your bodice masters, regardless of which master pattern you are using. For garments with a waistline seam, you can lengthen or shorten the skirt. The new base should be the same width as your hip-level guideline and parallel to the original base for a straight hem. The same applies in a princess seamline master or vertical seamline master; however, the base needs to be at least as wide as your hip-level measurement with ease.

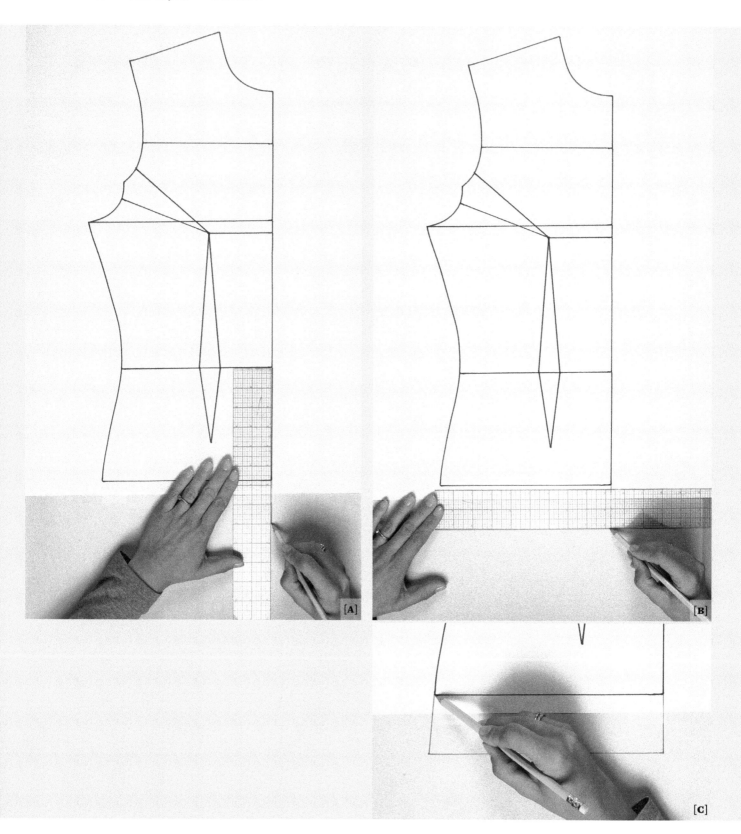

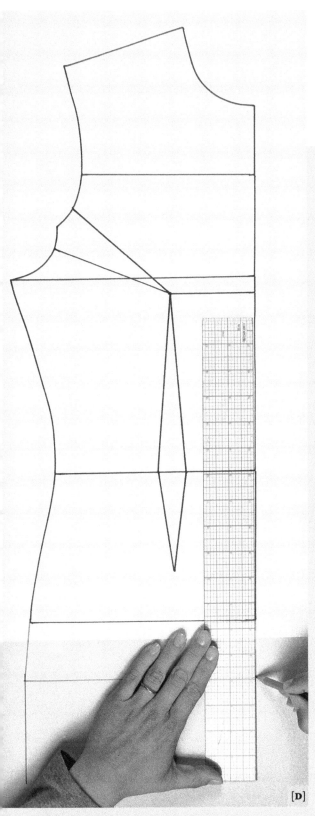

[D]

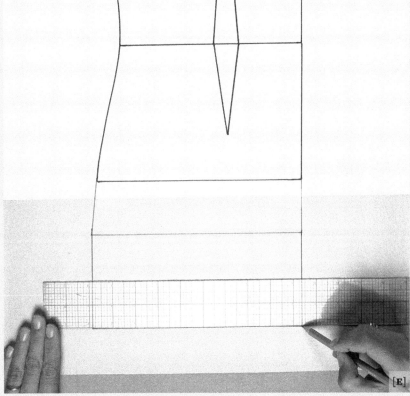

[E]

1

Lengthen the center front and back guidelines down to the level of your hip [A]. Skip to step 6 if the length of your master pattern is to the hip level or beyond.

2

Draw a horizontal guideline down from the waist to your hip-level guideline [B].

3

Extend your side seam until it intersects the hip-level guideline [C].

4

Repeat steps 2–3 for the back.

5

Measure the front and back hip-level guideline. Add the measurements together and then multiply by 2. This measurement should be at least 1" (2.5 cm) bigger than your body's measurement to factor in ease. Adjust the width of the master patterns at the side seams as needed.

Refer to photo [D] for steps 6 and 7.

6

Extend the center front guideline from the hip-level guideline to the desired length.

7

Extend the side straight down perpendicular to the hip-level guideline to the same length as the center front.

8

Connect the center front to the side. Make sure the measurement at the new base is the same as the hip-level guideline [E].

9

Repeat steps 6–8 for the back.

Center Back Seam Shaping

Many patterns have a straight center back from the neck or waist to the hem. However, the back of your body is not straight, regardless of your posture. Many designs can benefit from having a center back seam that has shape or contouring.

The shaping will be the most at the waistline and then blend back to the original center back portion at your fuller parts—the hip level below the waist and the bust or cross back above the waist. The amount taken away from the center back should be no more than ⅜" inch (1 cm) at the waist; any more than that and the back seam begins to get off grain. So that you don't make your garment any smaller, the amount of dart take-up will be reduced by the amount of back shaping. If you decide to do back shaping, it should be done right after tracing your master pattern. Note that this should be done only to the center back seam and not the front. It is best if the center front remains straight. This works on all garments.

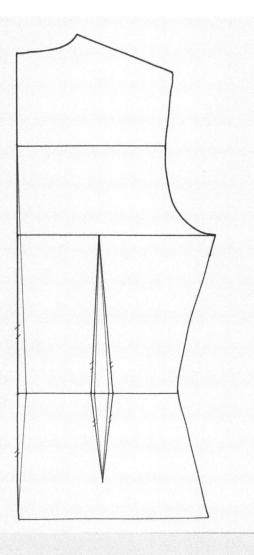

1
Trace the back master pattern.

2
Along your waistline, measure ⅜" (1 cm) from the center back toward the side seam. Mark this as your new center back point on the waistline.

3
Below the waist, connect the shaping to 1" (2.5 cm) above your hip-level guideline.

4
Above your waist, connect the shaping to either the bust guideline (allows for more room across a sleeved garment) or the cross back guideline, which is great for a fitted sleeveless garment.

5
Adjust the back dart so that it is smaller than the original by ⅜" (1 cm). If your original dart take-up was 1" (2.5 cm), your new dart take-up should be ⅝" (1.5 cm). Keep the dart center in the original position and bring each dart leg closer to the center by 3/16" (5 mm).

6
Make sure your grainline is still parallel to the original center back.

TIP

Remove back seam shaping by reversing these instructions. This gives you the option to cut back on the fold. But remember, you still need to be able to get into your garment somehow!

FRONT OR BACK OPENING

All garments can open or close on any seam. I encourage you to decide early in the process where you want your garment to close and choose the flat pattern methods to get you there. For example, dresses often close at the center back, making it a great place to highlight center back shaping. A jacket or blouse will close at the front, so use instructions for plackets and facings in the chapters ahead. Knowing how the garment will function may change where and how you want to use stylelines and shaping.

Sleeveless Bodices

Many fitting shell garments or master patterns are designed with sleeves. There is usually at least 2 inches (5.1 cm) of ease at the underarm of a fitting shell bodice. To simply eliminate the sleeves will leave you with gaping armholes that are not very fitted. Two adjustments should be done to any sleeveless design. Either follow these instructions for each and every sleeveless garment you design or make these adjustments and set up a sleeveless master pattern to use for all of your sleeveless designs.

Sleeveless Ease Adjustment

Reducing the ease at the base of the armhole will refine the look of a more tailored sleeveless garment. Since sleeveless garments do not restrict arm movement, you can fit the side seam a little more snugly to the body. (This adjustment can be ignored for a very relaxed fit sleevess garment, but make sure you're not revealing your undergarments more than you want to.)

Master Pattern Measurement	Front	+	Back	=	Multiply by	=	–	Full Body Measurement	= Total amount of ease	Divided by	= Amount of ease per pattern piece
Sample Bust	9" (23 cm)		8½" (21.6 cm)	17½" (44.6 cm)	x2	35" (89 cm)		33" (84 cm)	2" (5.1 cm)	÷4	½" (1.3 cm)
Bust											

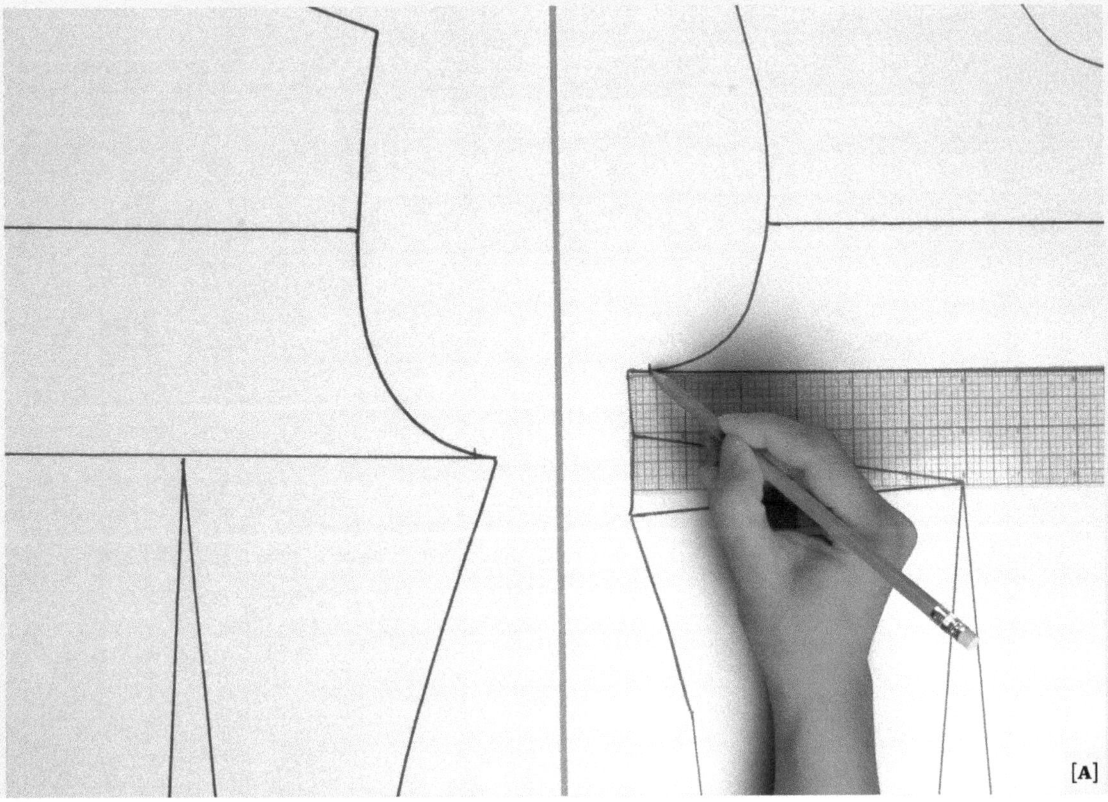

1
Refer to the chart above to determine how much ease is on your bust guideline.

2
Trace your front and back bodice master patterns.

3
Maintain a total of 1" (2.5 cm) ease at the bust guideline. Notice the above example determines 2" (5.1 cm) ease exists in the master pattern. Remove excess ease on bust guideline as necessary. To keep 1" (2.5 cm) ease, each side should still have ¼" (6 mm) ease [A].

[A]

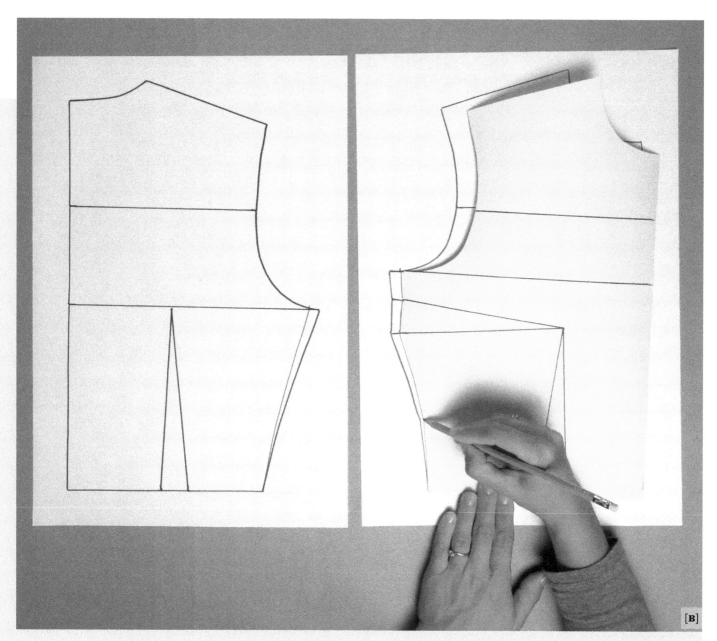

[B]

4
Blend from underarm
to the original waist
by placing your master
pattern in position at the
waist and pivot into the
new position on the bust
guideline to maintain the
original side shape [B].

5
Make a new back sleeve-
less master pattern.
Wait to create a new front
until you have read the
next section, Sleeveless
Armhole Dart (opposite).

Sleeveless Armhole Dart

Without an armhole dart, your sleeveless ease will fix only a certain amount of gaping. While wearing your sleeveless fitting shell, pinch out the excess armhole volume. The amount is typically a quarter to half the amount of the bust dart take-up. Although you may not be able to pin out the excess volume from armhole to the bust apex, do this on paper. Find fun and creative ways to consolidate your darts or princess stylelines.

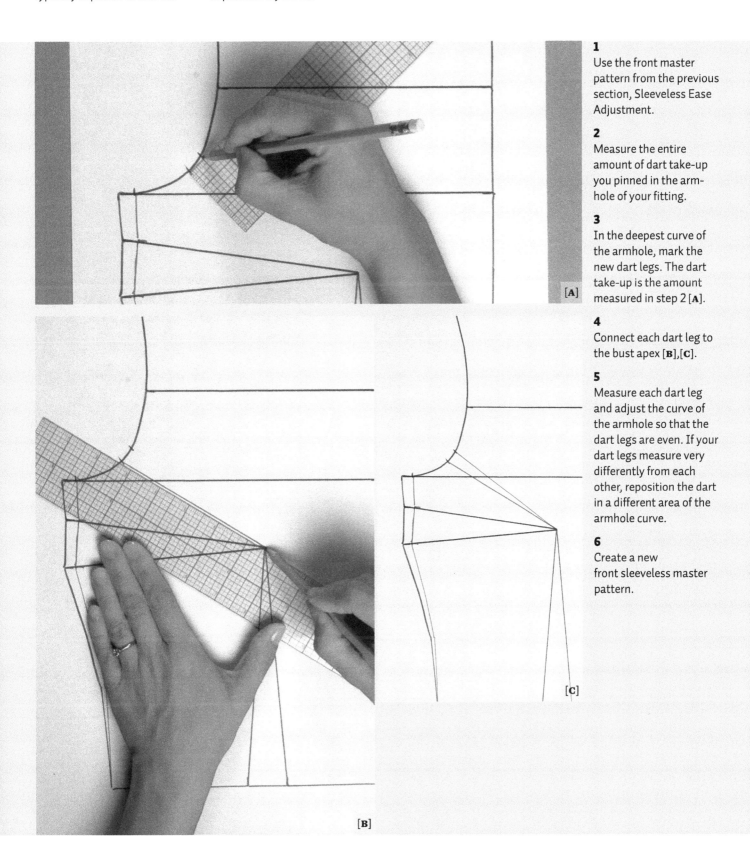

[A]

[B]

[C]

1
Use the front master pattern from the previous section, Sleeveless Ease Adjustment.

2
Measure the entire amount of dart take-up you pinned in the armhole of your fitting.

3
In the deepest curve of the armhole, mark the new dart legs. The dart take-up is the amount measured in step 2 [A].

4
Connect each dart leg to the bust apex [B],[C].

5
Measure each dart leg and adjust the curve of the armhole so that the dart legs are even. If your dart legs measure very differently from each other, reposition the dart in a different area of the armhole curve.

6
Create a new front sleeveless master pattern.

Bodice Design

There is an overwhelming number of design choices for tops. Choosing the right master pattern will allow the design to come together more easily.

—

Suggestions for master patterns, as well as alternative options, are given in each section. As you get more comfortable with the process, combine the drafting methods to create complex designs. The focus of this section will be sleeveless tops, but any of these exercises can be done on garments with sleeves, without making the sleeveless adjustments.

—

Review the section on Adding Ease (page 15) before designing new styles from your bodice master.

Changes to the Neckline

Making changes to the neckline can really change the character of the garment dramatically. An unflattering neckline can truly make or break a garment. There are two changes to the neckline. The first is lowering the neckline in the front or back, as low as you want to go! The other change is making the neckline wider while narrowing the shoulder seam.

Without proper drafting methods, the neckline can be too revealing at the bust and have excessive gaping. Each adjustment will be addressed separately but, of course, the methods can be combined. However, try these changes individually first and then play with combinations. These adjustments can be applied to any bodice master pattern, but make them first in the design process.

Wide Neckline

For a wider neckline, the changes are made to the shoulder seam, allowing more of the neck to show. A wide neckline may seem straight-forward, but because of the shape of our bodies and how we move, it needs a pattern adjustment. When you widen the front neckline, the back needs to become even wider.

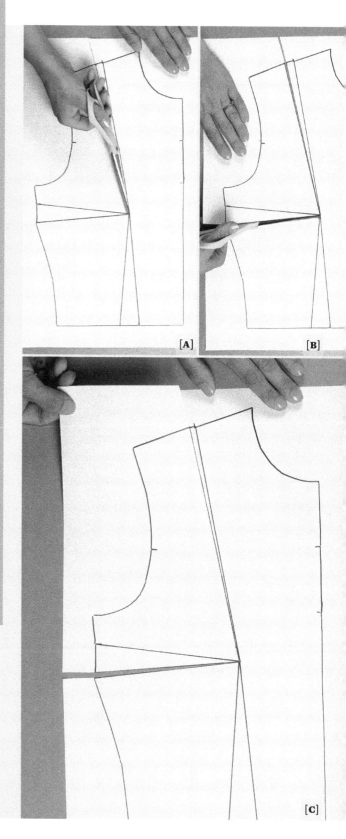

[A] [B] [C]

Your neckline lands in which portion of your shoulder seam	Extend back shoulder more than the front by this amount:
Original position	0
In the first quarter	¼" (6 mm)
In the second quarter	½" (1.3 cm)
In the third quarter	¾" (1.9 cm)
In the last quarter	1" (2.5 cm)

Q1
Q2
Q3
Q4

Original Position

1
Trace your chosen front bodice master pattern onto drafting paper.

2
If your bodice master pattern has a shoulder dart, manipulate it to another location to easily draw a smooth neckline shape. If you do not have a shoulder dart, skip to step 6.

3
Cut one leg of your shoulder dart from the pattern perimeter to your bust apex but not through it [A].

4
Cut one leg of your side dart from the pattern perimeter to your bust apex but not through it [B].

5
Tape the cut leg to the uncut leg of your shoulder dart, overlapping the dart take-up. This will open your side dart. Use dart manipulation or princess or empire seamlines to adjust this more to your liking after drafting your neckline [C].

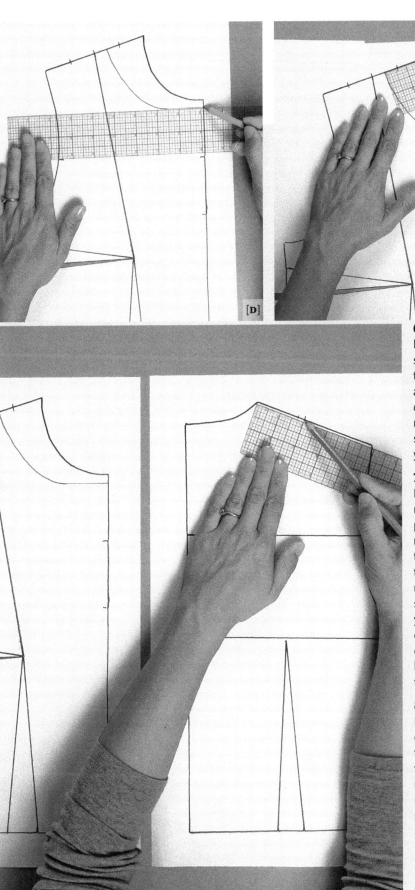

6
Draw in your neckline shape. Square off of the center front unless a V-shaped neckline is desired. Arc the neckline up to the shoulder seam in whatever shape you want [D].

7
Divide your shoulder measurement into four parts. Measure and record the distance from the original neckline to the new neckline. Determine what quarter of your shoulder measurement your new neckline is drawn in. Reference the chart on page 70 to see how much wider to make the back neckline [E].

8
Measure from the original back neckline the same distance from your original front neckline to the new neckline measurement plus the amount determined by the chart [F].

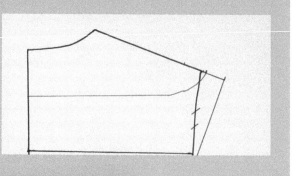

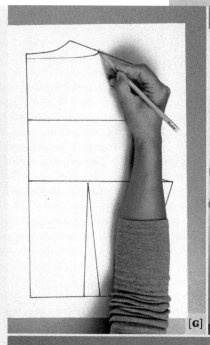

[G]

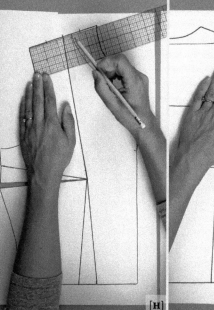

[H]

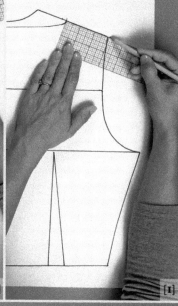

[I]

9
Draw in the desired shape of the back neckline. See the next chapter for necklines below the back bust guideline [G].

10
Measure the finished front shoulder seam length [H] and make sure the back shoulder seam is as wide [I].

You may need to extend your shoulder past the armhole and redraw a new armhole from the shoulder slope to the cross back guideline [J].

11
Continue to draft new stylelines and silhouettes.

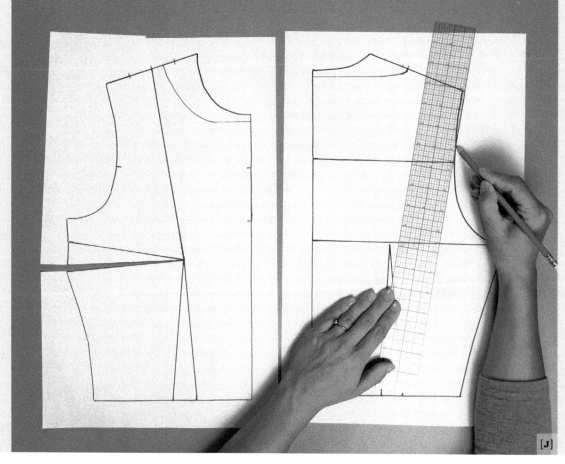

[J]

Deep Front Neckline

For a neckline that falls below the bust guideline, you'll need to add an extra dart. This dart will be drawn in along your neckline edge so that your garment does not hover above your bust but contours between your breasts at the center front. This additional dart can be converted into a dart manipulation or princess styleline as discussed in later chapters.

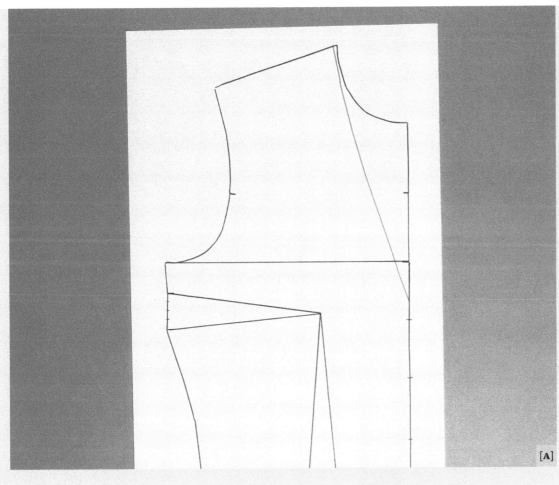

[A]

1
Trace your chosen front bodice master pattern onto drafting paper.

2
Draw in the shape of the desired neckline. Your neckline width should be at least 1" (2.5 cm) closer to center front than your bust apex. A neckline cut too close to your bust apex point will be too revealing [A].

3
How deep the neckline is determines the size of your additional dart. Follow the chart below to determine the size of your neckline dart.

Measure the length of your center front from bust guideline to waist. Divide this into four parts.

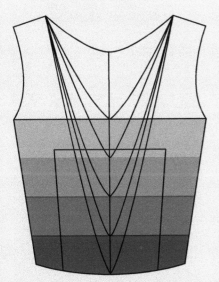

Your neckline falls:	Add a new dart with take-up this size:
At or above the bust guideline	0
In the first quarter	A quarter of your bust dart
In the second quarter	Half of your bust dart
In the third quarter	Three quarters of your bust dart
In the last quarter	Equal to your bust dart

4
Mark the new dart legs
on the neckline close to
the bust apex guideline.
The chart on the previous
page determines the
dart take-up [**B**].

5
Connect the dart legs to
the bust apex [**C**].

6
See later chapters
to transfer the dart
take-up with dart
manipulation or princess
seamline designs.

[B]

[C]

Deep Back Neckline

A back neckline that dips below
the bust guideline offers more
ease in the garment because
the fabric is not taut across your
back. A simple side-seam adjustment can be made to correct for
this. Make these changes only
to the back, not the front.

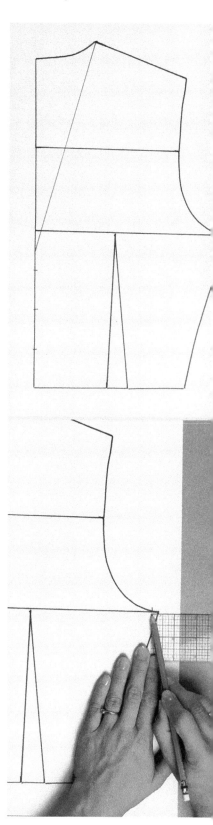

1
Trace your back bodice master pattern onto drafting paper.

2
Draw in the shape of the desired back neckline [A].

3
On the bust guideline, measure and record the space between the original center back to the new neckline.

4
Shave this amount off of the side seam at the bust guideline [B].

5
Use the back master pattern to redraw the new side seam from the bust guideline down to the waist. Notice the waist measurement has not been made smaller [C].

6
Redraw the armhole if necessary so that the base of it is on the bust guideline [D].

A back neckline dart can be taken in the fitting if the back neckline gapes away from the body. The neckline dart will be drafted similar to a front neckline, but instead of connecting to the bust apex it will connect to the perimeter of the pattern piece, usually at the side seam or the armhole. Cut one dart leg and place it on top of the other dart to manipulate the dart out of the pattern.

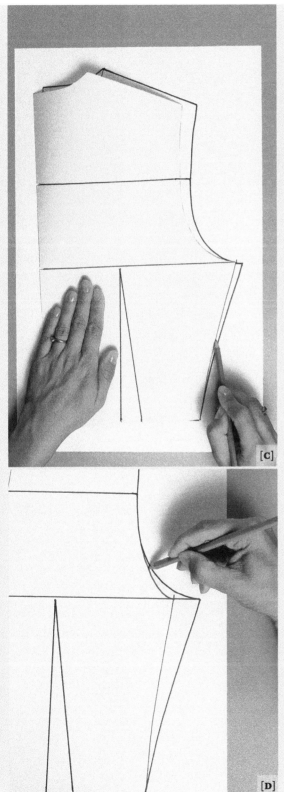

[A]

[C]

[B]

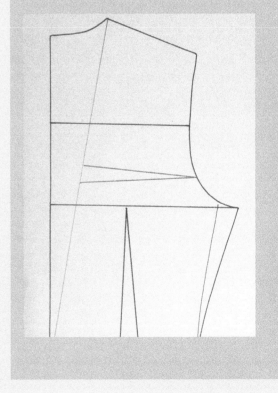

[D]

Dart Manipulation

Dart manipulation gives you the freedom to take some or all of your darts and move them to new and more exciting positions while still achieving the same great fit of your master pattern. There are endless design possibilities. You can manipulate all the darts into one new dart or multiple new darts. Darts can also be converted into pleats, gathers, and tucks. For a more relaxed fit, you can ignore darts as well. However, do not ignore your side/bust dart because it will not fit well and the front side length will not match your back side length.

Dart manipulation techniques are easiest to start with on a garment with a waistline seam. Once you have experimented, try combining a dart manipulation with an empire styleline or princess seamline. Also, the waist dart can be ignored, eliminating the need for a waistline seam.

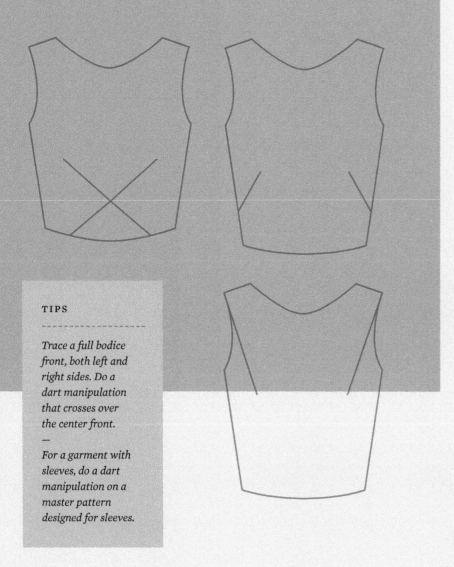

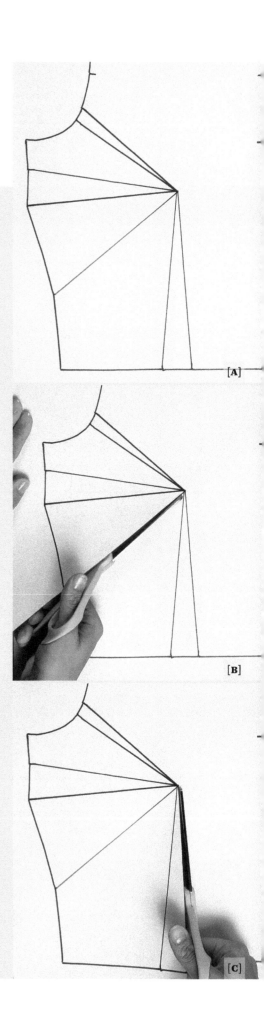

[A]

[B]

[C]

TIPS

- - - - - - - - - - - - - - - - - - - -

Trace a full bodice front, both left and right sides. Do a dart manipulation that crosses over the center front.

—

For a garment with sleeves, do a dart manipulation on a master pattern designed for sleeves.

TIP

Convert all darts to an existing dart. Use the original dart legs, not just the cut leg.

1

Trace your chosen front bodice master pattern onto drafting paper. Make any changes to your neckline. Mark your bust apex and all dart legs.

2

Decide where the new dart will be created. Draw a line from the bust apex to the perimeter of the pattern [**A**].

3

Cut the new dart line from the perimeter to the bust apex but not through it [**B**].

4

Cut any one dart leg from the perimeter to the bust apex but not through it. To keep your work manageable, cut one dart leg at a time [**C**].

5

Close the dart by moving the cut dart leg to the uncut dart leg, overlapping the dart take-up. Tape to secure [**D**].

Notice that the new dart position begins to open and forms a new dart take-up!

6

Repeat for all the remaining darts that are to be manipulated [**E**].

7

Place paper behind the newly created dart and secure with tape [**F**].

[**D**]

[**E**]

[**F**]

TIP

Ignore the waist dart for a more relaxed fit.

TIP

If you have a large bust cup size, D or larger, create a design with two darts so that the darts legs are more stable and more flattering on your figure.

Refer to photo [G] for steps 8 and 9.

TIP

If your dart take-up is more than 2" (5.1 cm), convert the dart take-up to seam allowance on the dart legs to reduce bulk in the finished sewn garment.

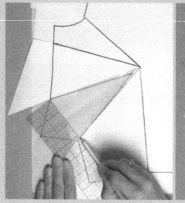

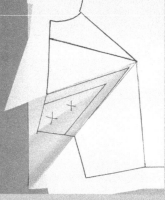

[G]

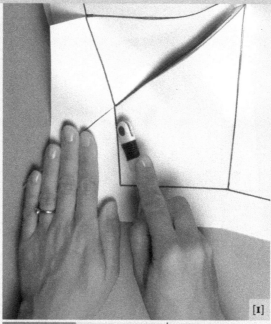

[I]

8

If desired, move the bust apex dart point toward the perimeter of the pattern. This moves the dart point slightly away from the fullest point of the bust.

9

Connect the legs of the dart to the original or adjusted bust apex point. Notch each dart leg and awl punch ½" (1.3 cm) away from the dart point toward the perimeter.

10

Fold the dart leg closest to the side or bottom of the pattern and stack it on top of the other dart leg [H].

11

With a tracing wheel, trace the shape of the pattern perimeter through the fold [I].

Unfold and draw the traced shape [J].

12

Draw your grainline parallel to center front. Label your front pattern "Cut 1 on fold of self fabric" or continue to draft a front closure with collar.

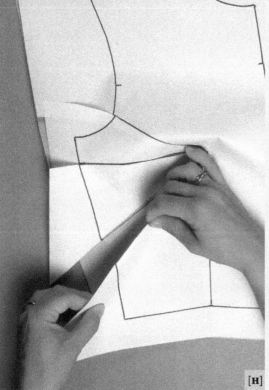

[H]

[J]

Darts as Tucks

You can create tucks instead of marking and sewing your darts from the perimeter all the way to the bust apex. Tucks are darts sewn partially from the perimeter, not all the way to the dart point. The drafting is mostly the same as for dart manipulation; however, you may want more than one tuck in your pattern.

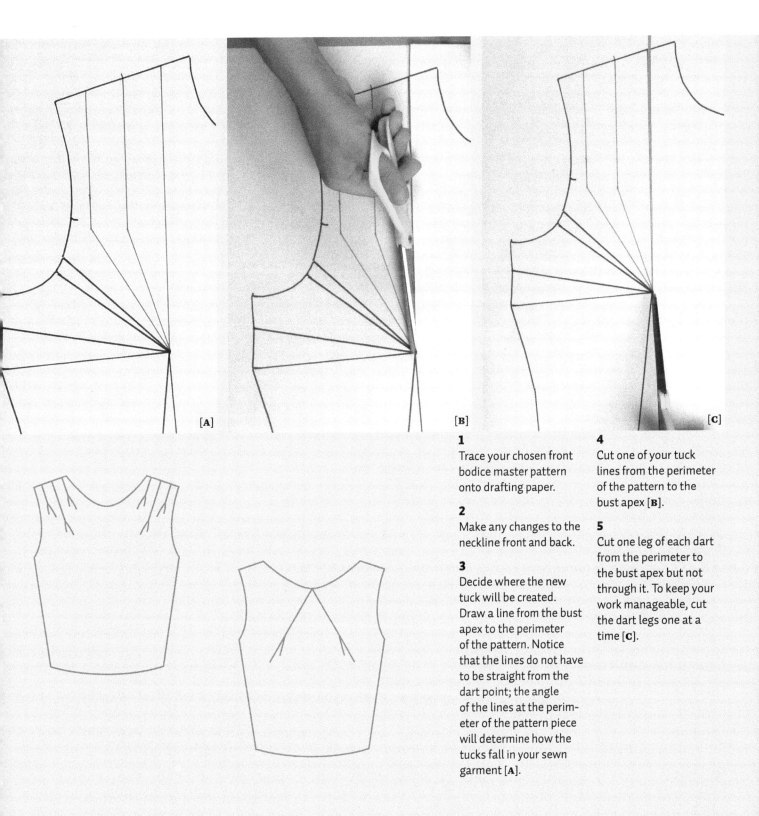

[A]   [B]   [C]

1
Trace your chosen front bodice master pattern onto drafting paper.

2
Make any changes to the neckline front and back.

3
Decide where the new tuck will be created. Draw a line from the bust apex to the perimeter of the pattern. Notice that the lines do not have to be straight from the dart point; the angle of the lines at the perimeter of the pattern piece will determine how the tucks fall in your sewn garment [A].

4
Cut one of your tuck lines from the perimeter of the pattern to the bust apex [B].

5
Cut one leg of each dart from the perimeter to the bust apex but not through it. To keep your work manageable, cut the dart legs one at a time [C].

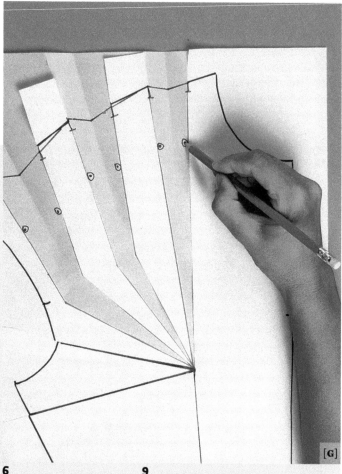

[G]

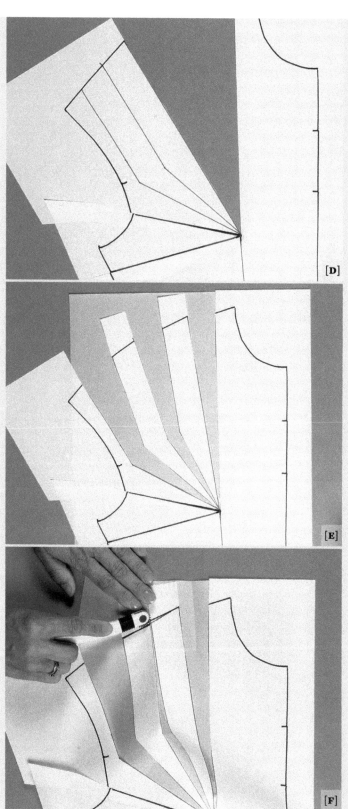

[D]

[E]

[F]

6

Close the dart by moving the cut dart leg to the uncut dart leg, overlapping the dart take-up. Repeat for all darts to be manipulated [**D**].

*Refer to photo [**E**] for steps 7 and 8.*

7

If you have more than one tuck line, cut the remaining tuck lines and distribute the take-up across them. The distribution can be equal or unequal.

8

Add paper behind all tuck insertions. Tape to secure.

9

Fold the paper the way you want your tucks folded in your sewn garment. You may need to redraw the original seam shape by trimming angular spikes on the pattern perimeter and filling in the perimeter in shallow spots [**F**].

10

With a tracing wheel, trace the shape of the pattern perimeter through the folded paper. Unfold and draw the traced shape.

11

Notch each tuck leg and awl punch along the tuck line to the point you want to sew the tuck down. If you want your tucks relaxed from the perimeter, then you only need notches [**G**].

Darts as Gathers

Gathers can create nice bust shaping and feel like a more relaxed fit. Gathers take up space, unlike tucks that can be folded out tidily.

TIPS

Use multiple gather lines to spread fullness over a larger area.

Gather to a styleline. Place the notches across the styleline to indicate the space the gathers will be sewn to.

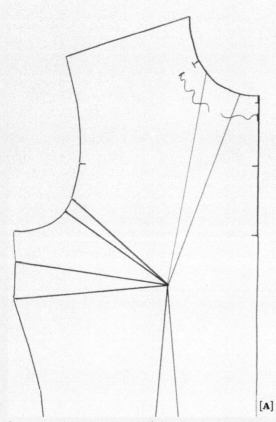

[A]

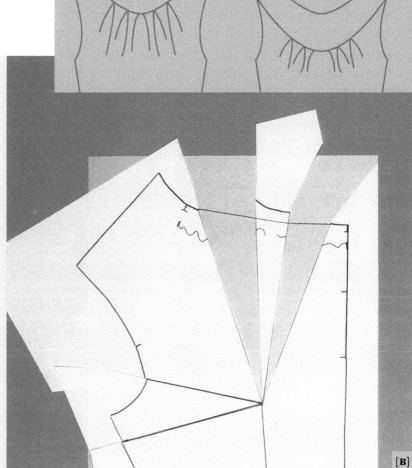

[B]

1
Trace your chosen front bodice master pattern onto drafting paper.

2
Make the desired neckline changes.

Refer to photo [A] for steps 3 and 4.

3
Draw a line from your bust apex to the perimeter of the pattern in the center position where you want your gathers to appear.

4
Place notches ½" to 2" (1.3 to 5.1 cm) to each side of the gather line. Measure and note the space between notches before making insertions. This will be the space the gathers will be sewn to. Gathering takes up more space in a heavyweight fabric than in a lighter weight fabric.

Refer to photo [B] for steps 5–11.

5
Cut your gather line from the perimeter of the pattern to the bust apex.

6
Cut one leg of each dart from the perimeter to the bust apex but not through it. To keep your work manageable, cut the dart legs one at a time.

7
Close the dart by moving the cut dart leg to the uncut dart leg, overlapping the dart take-up. Tape to secure.

8
Repeat for all of the remaining darts.

9
If using more than one gather line, cut the remaining gather line(s) and distribute the take-up evenly across them.

10
Place paper behind all gather lines. Tape to secure.

11
Draw a line from the beginning of the gather to the end in a nice soft curve, possibly trimming angular spikes on the pattern perimeter and filling in the perimeter in shallow spots.

12
Mark the pattern for the amount that these will be gathered to as determined in step 4.

Princess Seamlines

A princess seamline is a long, continuous, vertical styleline from the top of the bodice all the way to the hem of a garment without the need for a waistline seam. Princess seamlines that are softly curved are more figure flattering than darts, which can become cone shaped. Depending on the line of a princess seam, the illusion of curves enhances or minimizes curves of the body.

Your princess seamlines will fit much better if the styleline passes through or within ½ to 1 inch (1.2 to 2.5 cm) of your bust apex. The more fitted the garment, the closer the seamline should be to your bust apex. The more relaxed the garment, the farther away the seamline can be from the bust apex.

Great jacket and dress patterns can be created in this section. Feel free to shorten or lengthen your skirt pattern piece from the master pattern (see page 62).

If you are working with a bodice and skirt master pattern, make sure the waist measurement of the bodice is equal to the waist measurement of the skirt, because the amounts of ease can be different. If they are not the same measurement, refer to Aligning the Master Bodice and Skirt Combination, page 54, for adjustment options.

Working from a Bodice and Skirt Master

The bodice and skirt master patterns can be joined with a vertical princess seam that eliminates the need for the waist seam.

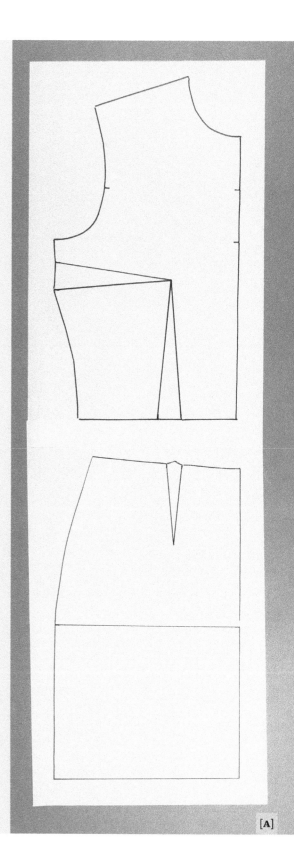

[A]

Do not make a princess style-line from the armhole curved above the bust. It looks funny and makes the bust appear to be in the wrong place. A seamline that is straight from the armhole to or near the bust apex will appear more curved when sewn and worn.

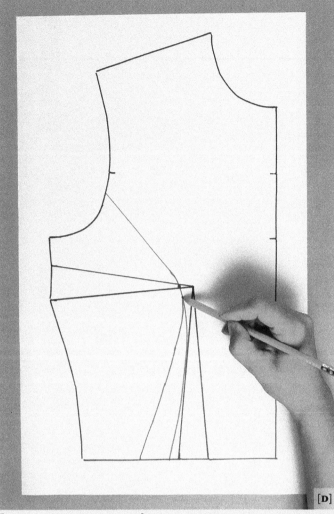

[D]

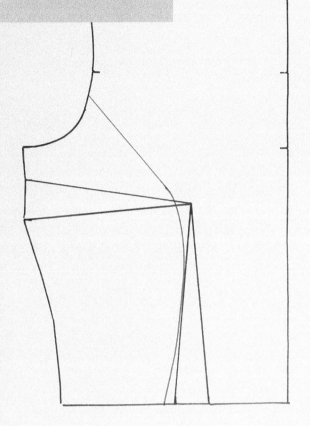

[B]

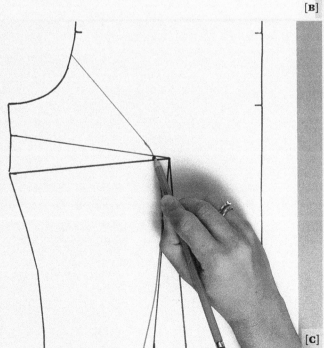

[C]

1
Trace your front bodice and your front skirt master patterns onto separate drafting paper [A].

2
Make any changes to the front and back neckline. Make any changes to the length of the front and back skirt pattern.

3
On the bodice pattern, draw a styleline from the perimeter of the neck, shoulder, or armhole, passing near or through the bust apex and ending on the perimeter at the waistline [B].

4
Move your bust apex point onto the princess styleline, level with its original position [C].

5
Measure the waist dart take-up on your bodice master pattern and mark this distance from your princess seamline toward the side seam. Redraw a new waist dart so that one leg is your princess seamline and the second leg is closer to the side seam and blends to the bust apex. The dart legs can be slightly curved [D].

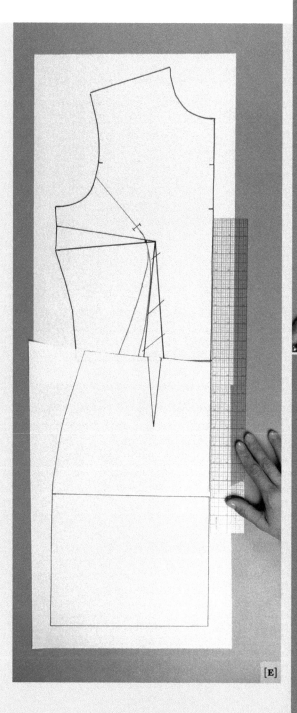

[E]

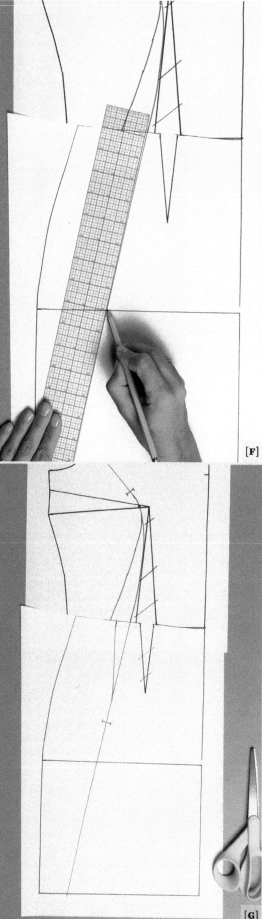

[F]

[G]

Refer to photo [E] for steps 6 and 7.

6

Cut away excess paper from the skirt master pattern's waistline.

7

Attach the bodice to the skirt at the waist so that the center front guidelines stay straight. Tape the skirt to the bodice only between the center front and the princess seamline. The skirt side may overlap with the bodice side.

8

Draw a continuation of the princess seamline all the way to the hem of the skirt [F].

Refer to photo [G] for steps 9 and 10.

9

Measure the waist dart take-up on your skirt master pattern and mark this distance from your skirt's princess seamline toward the side seam. Redraw a new waist dart so that one leg is your princess seamline and the second leg is closer to the side seam and blends to the original depth of the dart. The dart legs can be slightly curved.

10

Place notches across the princess styleline near the bust apex and somewhere in the skirt section.

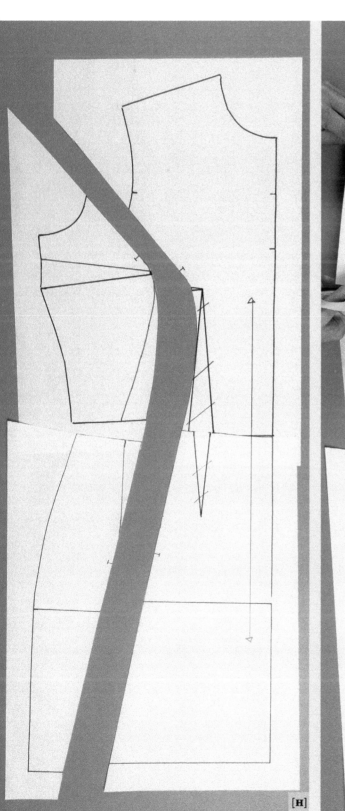

11
Cut along the princess seamline of the skirt and bodice [**H**].

12
Place the grainline parallel to center front and label as "Cut 1 on fold of self fabric." Set the center front piece aside. This should be one continuous piece from neck to hem.

13
Cut one leg of the side dart from the side toward the bust apex but not through it; just a small bit of paper will be tethered together [**I**].

[H]

[I]

TIP

----

*Add a front closure.
Instructions for plackets
and facings are in the
next chapter, Collars
and Closures.*

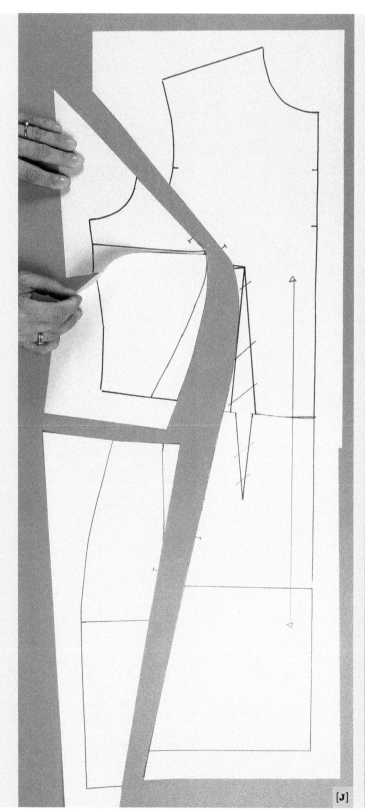

[J]

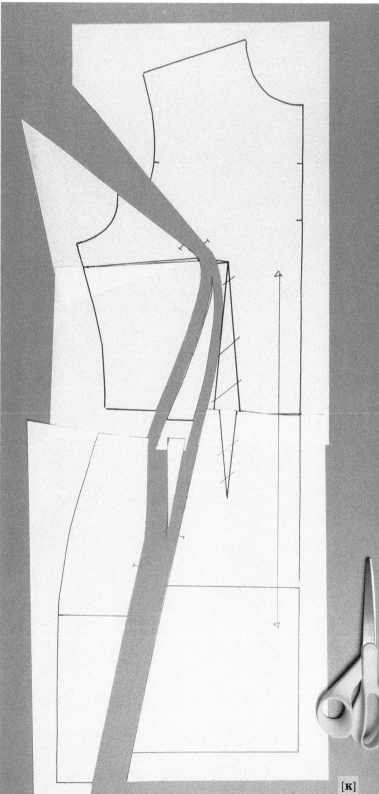

[K]

14

Close the dart by moving the cut dart leg to the uncut dart leg, overlapping the dart take-up [**J**].

15

Repeat steps 13 and 14 for all the remaining darts, including the neckline dart on the center front piece, if one exists.

16

Cut the waist dart away from the side front of the skirt and the bodice [**K**].

17

Connect the side front skirt to the side front bodice at the princess line and waistline. Tape to secure [**L**].

18

Draw a grainline perpendicular to the hip-level guideline and label "Cut 2 of self fabric."

19

Repeat for the back.

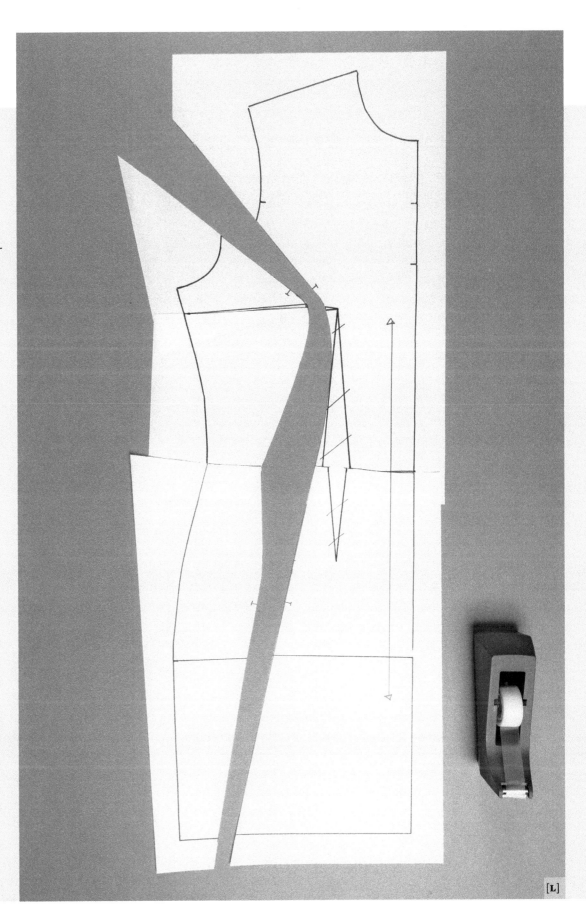

[**L**]

Working from a Princess Seamline Master

Your master pattern likely informs a certain style princess seamline but it can easily be changed. The following instructions show you how to move the shaping of darts from one location to another.

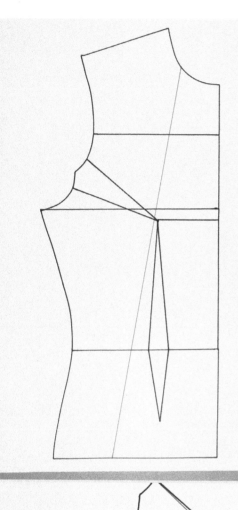

[A]

1
Trace your chosen princess seamline master onto drafting paper. Make any changes to the neckline and length as desired.

2
Draw a styleline from the perimeter of the neck, shoulder, or armhole, passing near or through the bust apex and ending on the perimeter of the pattern base [A].

Refer to photo [B] for steps 3 and 4.

3
Move your bust apex point onto the princess styleline, level with its original position.

4
Measure the waist dart take-up on your master pattern and mark this distance from your princess seamline toward the side seam. Redraw a new top of the waist dart so that one leg is your princess seamline and the second leg is closer the side seam and blends to the bust apex. Redraw a new bottom portion of the waist dart so that one leg is your princess seamline and the second leg is closer the side seam and blends to the original depth of the dart.

The dart legs can be slightly curved.

5
Repeat steps 10–12 from Working from a Bodice and Skirt Master (page 82).

6
Cut one leg of the bust shaping dart from the side toward the bust apex but not through it; just a small bit of paper will be tethered together.

7
Close the dart by moving the cut dart leg to the uncut dart leg, overlapping the dart take-up.

8
Repeat steps 6 and 7 for all the remaining darts, including the neckline dart on the center front piece, if one exists.

9
Cut the waist dart away from the side front pattern.

10
Draw a grainline perpendicular to the hip-level guideline and label "Cut 2 of self fabric."

11
Repeat for the back.

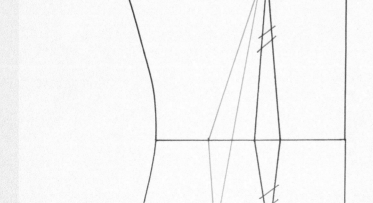

[B]

Empire Seamlines

An empire line is a horizontal seamline that falls below the bust and above the waist. It can be paired with dart manipulation, princess seamlines, and skirt techniques.

The empire line can be quite fitted. While wearing your sewn fitting master pattern, you can widen the waist darts under the bust to create a more body-conscious fit. A great location for an empire seam is where the waist darts are the widest.

These instructions are written for a bodice and skirt master pattern. If you started a princess seamline master pattern, you can make the same changes to the waist darts, as in steps 1 and 2. Then simply draw a horizontal styleline across your bodice master.

1
While wearing your fitting shell, adjust your waist dart so that it is snugger under the bust but maintains some wearable ease.

2
Trace your bodice master pattern.

3
Measure down from the bust apex to determine where the waist dart was made wider. Measure the entire amount of dart take-up you pinned out in your fitting. Mark this information onto your pattern piece. It can be helpful to mark this with an awl punch on your master patterns to reference later [**A**].

4
Draw your empire styleline, a horizontal styleline at or near where the waist dart adjustment has been made [**B**].

*Refer to photo [**C**] for steps 5–7.*

5
Draw a continuation of the center front guideline below the waistline.

6
Trace the front skirt master pattern. Cut away excess paper from the waistline.

7
Connect the waistline of the skirt and bodice master patterns at the side seams. Position the center front of the skirt master pattern on the drawn extension of the bodice center front. Tape to secure. Measure the gap between the bodice and skirt waistlines at the center front.

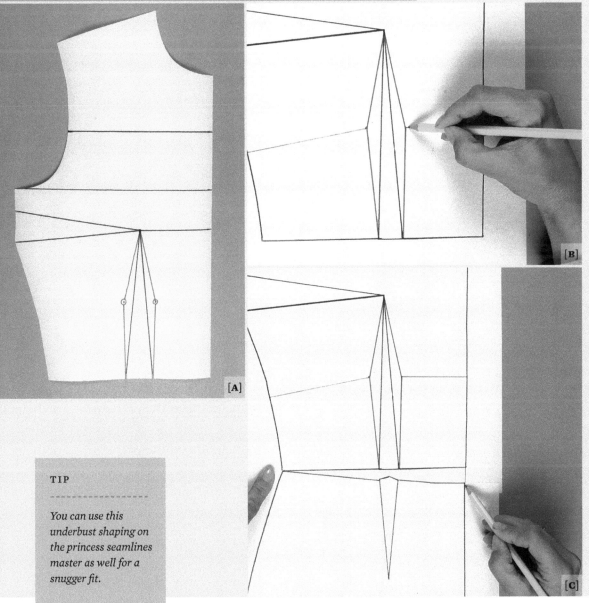

[A]

[B]

[C]

TIP

You can use this underbust shaping on the princess seamlines master as well for a snugger fit.

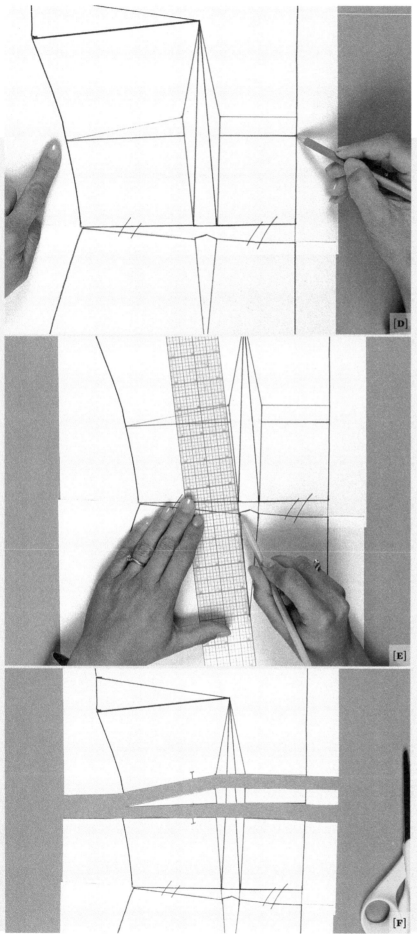

[D]

[E]

[F]

8
Draw the same size gap down from the empire styleline, connecting the center front to the side seam. The original gap on the waistline seam can be ignored [D].

9
Place a notch across the gap of the empire style-line, as the new gap will be cut away from the pattern piece.

Refer to photo [E] for steps 10 and 11.

10
Connect your dart legs straight through the gap at the empire styleline.

11
Connect the dart legs between the bodice and skirt at the original waistline.

12
Cut along the empire styleline, separating the bodice from the skirt. Cut away the gap that you drew in below the empire styleline and discard [F].

13
Repeat for the back.

> **TIP**
> - - - - - - - - - - - - - - - -
> *Do a dart manipu-lation or a princess seamline design in addition to the empire styleline.*

All-in-One Neckline and Armhole Facing

I love an all-in-one facing. It finishes off both the neckline and the armhole at once. When they are sewn separately, you often have a facing that wants to pop out of your finished garment. There are times when you need only an armhole facing, like when you have a collar. Or, if you have a sleeve, you may need only a neckline facing. Modify these instructions to suit your needs.

1
After you have drafted your bodice pattern pieces, draw in a shape of the facing that is 1½" to 3" (3.8 to 7.6 cm) down from the center front and the base of the armhole. The space in between these two reference points should curve around the bust apex but not pass through or below it [**A**].

2
On another sheet of paper, trace the facing pattern piece. On the facing pattern piece, trim away ¹⁄₁₆" to ⅛" (2 to 3 mm) from the neckline and armholes. This will keep the facing hidden inside on the finished garment [**B**],[**C**].

3
Cut your facing pattern pieces as your bodice pieces. Grainlines should be parallel to the center front or center back.

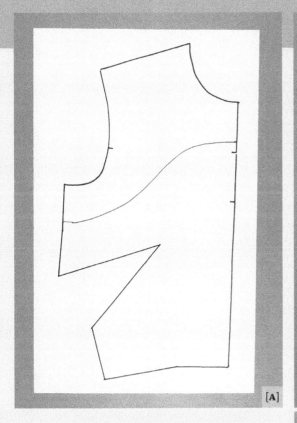

[A]

[B]

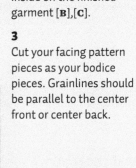

[C]

TIP

If you have princess seamlines and have already separated the patterns, tape the princess seamline together between the shoulder and the armhole before drawing in your facing.

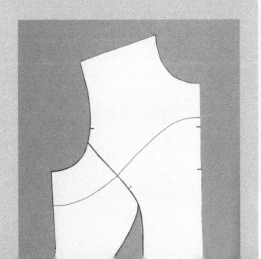

TIPS

If your neckline is very low, you may want to face the entire bodice.

—

Facings should be interfaced!

CHAPTER 5

Collars and Closures

The addition of a simple collar will affect where and how you want your garment to close and the finish of the neckline. This chapter is meant to build on top of the Bodice Design chapter.

—

Start designing elements from the previous chapter and learn to add more complex elements in this one. Adding a collar will change the dynamic and the function of the garment.

Closure Essentials

Garments that close with methods other than a zipper need to be drafted with an extension allowing the garment to overlap. This allows for placement of such closures as buttons, snaps, hooks and eyes, or any other closure you dream up.

Typically, your closure will be patterned off the center front guideline so that you can easily get in and out of your garments, but rules are meant to be broken.

The two most common ways to allow for this overlap are with a placket or a facing. A placket is an extension on the body of the garment and folds to the inside, finishing the edge of the garment. A placket is almost always sewn with buttons or snaps and has topstitching details.

A faced garment has an extension on the body of the garment that is sewn to a facing to finish the edge. Facings often lack topstitching and sometimes even closures. A facing also sews nicely to a lining.

Buttons and Buttonholes

Before patterning a facing or placket, you will need to determine not only the size of the button you will be using but the orientation of the buttonhole. To create a garment with snaps, your patterning will be the same as a button of the same size, however, you will not need to include buttonholes.

Placket

A placket allows the right and left side of a garment to overlap and gives space for buttons, snaps, or hooks. They are usually on the front of a garment. Plackets are a more casual alternative to a facing and they work well in an unlined garment. The drawback to a placket is that it finishes only the center front edge, requiring a separate neckline treatment such as a collar, facing, or trim.

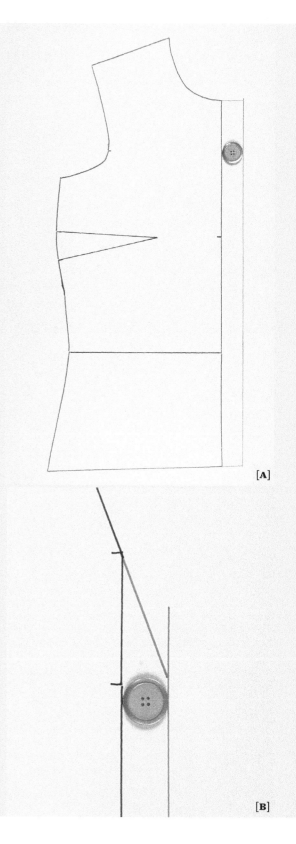

[A]

[B]

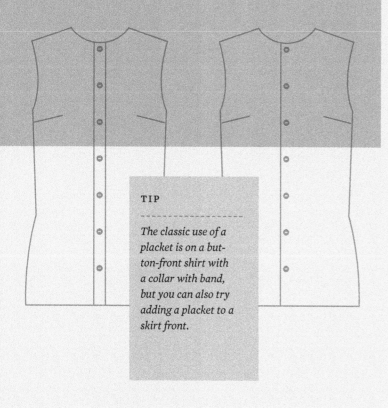

> **TIP**
>
> *The classic use of a placket is on a button-front shirt with a collar with band, but you can also try adding a placket to a skirt front.*

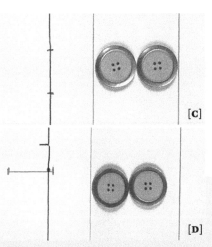

[C]

[D]

1
Trace your chosen front bodice master pattern or bodice design pattern onto drafting paper.

2
Decide on the size button you will use.

3
Draw a vertical line away from the center front that extends the diameter of your button. This is your button extension. Mark as a foldline. On a shallow neckline, the extension is perpendicular to the center front [A]. On a V-neckline, just continue the slope of the neckline through the extension [B].

4
Decide on vertical or horizontal buttonholes.

5
For vertical buttonholes, extend your pattern beyond the button extension foldline double your button width [C].

For horizontal buttonholes, extend your pattern beyond the foldline by double your button width plus ¼" (6 mm) [D].

6
Fold your paper to the back of your pattern on the button extension foldline. With a tracing wheel, draw the shape of the neckline and hem through the folded paper. Unfold and draw the traced shape. This is your self facing [E].

7
Notch your button extension foldline and center front at the neckline and hem [F],[G].

8
On a new sheet of paper, trace the shape of the button-extension foldline and the self facing. This is the interfacing pattern piece for both sides of the bodice front.

Place the grainline parallel to the center front and label the pattern "Cut 2 interfacing."

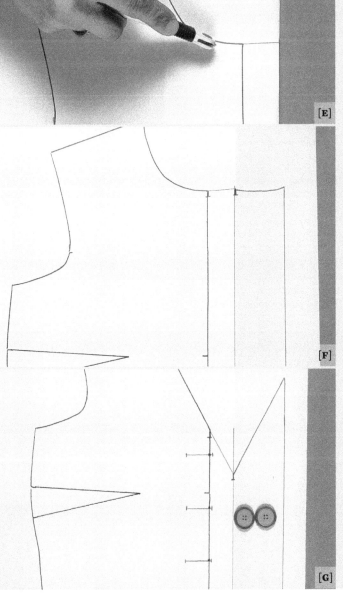

[E]

[F]

[G]

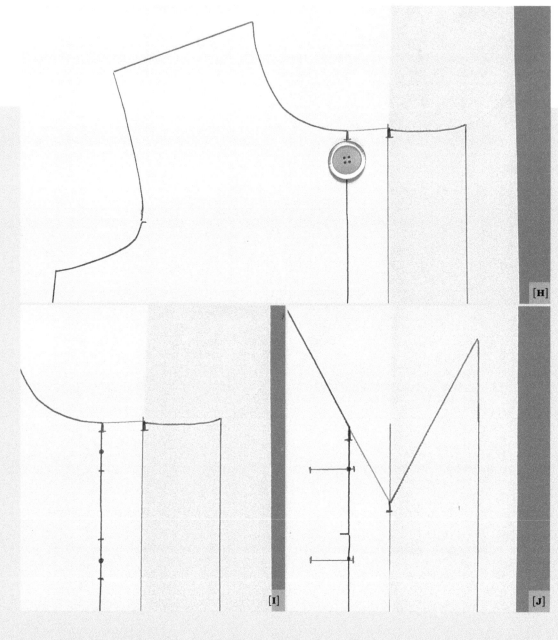

9

Place your buttons on the center front guideline. The center of the top button should be ¼" (6 mm) down from the neckline edge plus half the button's diameter. Decide where the bottom button will be; for a blouse, measure up from the base about 4" (10.2 cm). Fill in the space between evenly with the number of buttons desired. Mark button placement with awl punches [**H**].

10

Place your buttonholes.

For vertical buttonholes, put half the buttonhole above the button placement and half below [**I**].

For horizontal buttonholes, measure ⅛" (3 mm) from the center front toward the button extension foldline. Then, from the center front into the body of your garment, draw the width of the button [**J**].

[**H**]

[**I**]

[**J**]

BUTTON TIPS

Women's garments lap right over left, meaning buttonholes are placed on the right side, buttons on the left side. Men's garments lap left over right.

It is a good idea to have a button at the bust apex guideline. You can determine your spacing from your top button to the bust apex guideline. Then repeat this spacing to about 4" (10.2 cm) above the base.

For buttons bigger than 1" (2.5 cm) in diameter, use horizontal buttonholes. Horizontal buttonholes are more secure and will not pop open.

To make vertical buttonholes less prone to popping open, place the buttonhole just ⅛" (3 mm) above the button position and the full diameter of the button below.

A buttonhole should be about ⅛" (3 mm) bigger than your button so that you can easily button and unbutton your garment.

Facing

A facing is a universal pattern term for any pattern piece that finishes off a garment's edge and does not show on the outside. You have already seen an all-in-one neckline facing and a waistline facing; this is just a variation for a jacket, blouse, or dress with a center front closure. A facing is an alternative finish to a placket on a garment. Jackets are the most common place to see facings. It allows you to have the fashion fabric go back into the body of the garment on the inside and can join nicely to the lining. A facing often serves as a jacket lapel. Facings should always be interfaced.

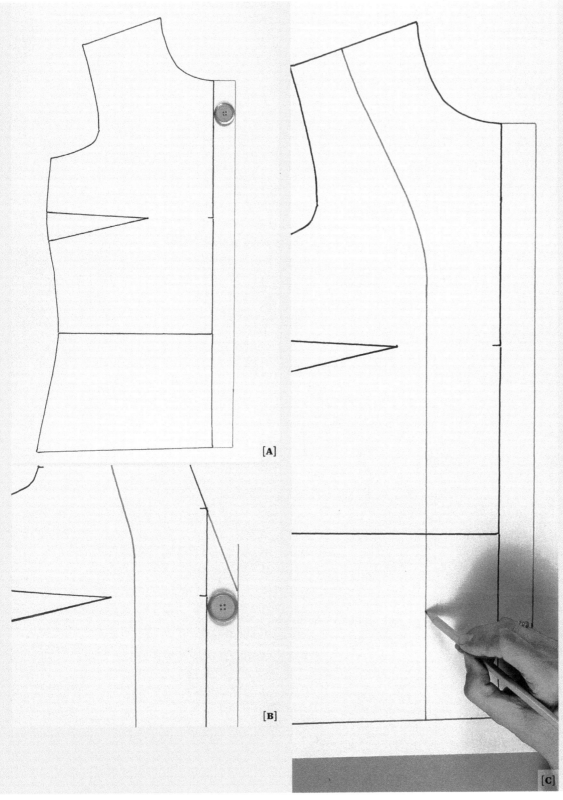

[A]

[B]

[C]

1
Trace your chosen front bodice master pattern or use a bodice design pattern.

2
Decide on the size of button you will use.

3
Draw a vertical line away from center front that extends the diameter of your button. This is your button extension. On a shallow neckline, the extension is perpendicular to the center front [A]. On a V-neckline, just continue the slope of the neckline through the extension [B].

Refer to photo [C] for steps 4 and 5.

4
On the self pattern piece, measure from the neckline across the shoulder the desired width of the facing, 1½" to 3" (3.8 to 7.6 cm). Measure from the base at the center front toward the side seam the desired width of the facing at the base—again 1½" to 3" (3.8 to 7.6 cm).

5
Connect these two reference points in a shallow curve. The space in between these two reference points should curve around the bust apex, not pass over it. When possible, the facing should not include any darts or shaped seaming.

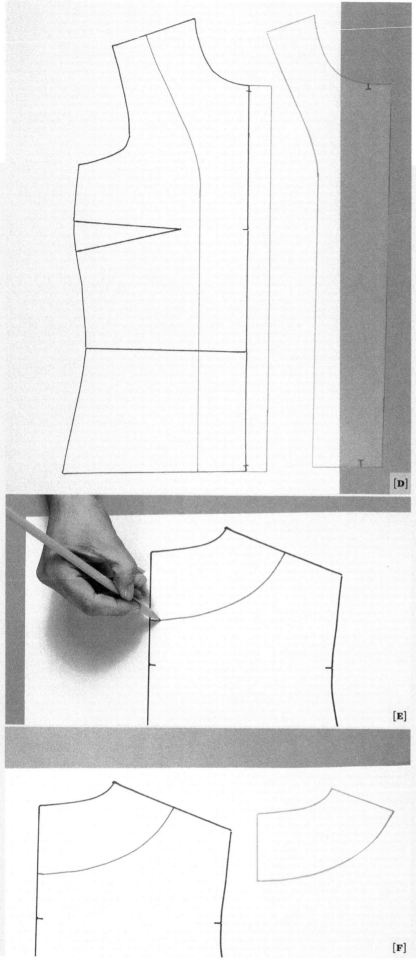

[D]

[E]

[F]

6

On a new sheet of paper, trace the shape of your facing [**D**].

7

The facing goes all the way to the base, including hem allowance. If you have not added hem allowance to your garment yet, do so now. See page 166 on hem allowances.

8

Mark the grainline parallel to the center front and label the pattern piece "Cut 2 self and interfacing."

9

On the back bodice, measure from the neckline across the shoulder the same distance the front facing was drafted. Measure down from the neck on the center back guideline the same distance. Connect these two points in a soft curve [**E**].

10

On a new sheet of paper, trace the pattern piece for your back neck facing [**F**].

11

Draw the grainline parallel to the center back. Label the pattern piece "Cut 1 on fold of self fabric and interfacing."

TIP

A collared and lined jacket can have a back neckline facing but does not need one. An unlined or collarless jacket must have a back neckline facing.

Collar Anatomy

These diagrams help illustrate the differences between a flat collar and a standing collar. Refer to this illustration to identify the names of the different collar parts.

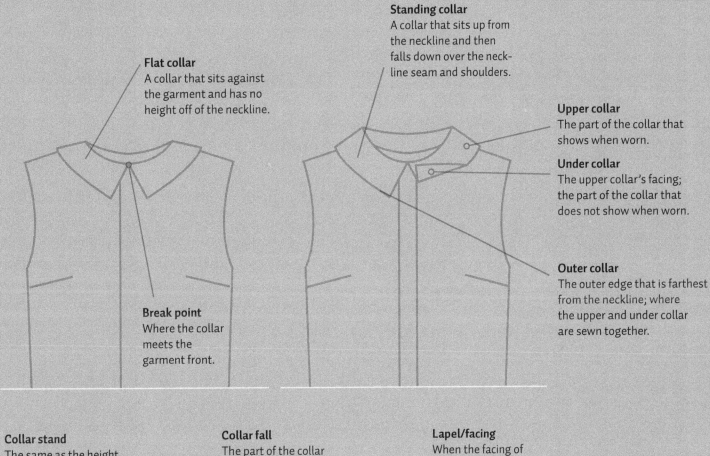

Flat collar
A collar that sits against the garment and has no height off of the neckline.

Standing collar
A collar that sits up from the neckline and then falls down over the neckline seam and shoulders.

Upper collar
The part of the collar that shows when worn.

Under collar
The upper collar's facing; the part of the collar that does not show when worn.

Outer collar
The outer edge that is farthest from the neckline; where the upper and under collar are sewn together.

Break point
Where the collar meets the garment front.

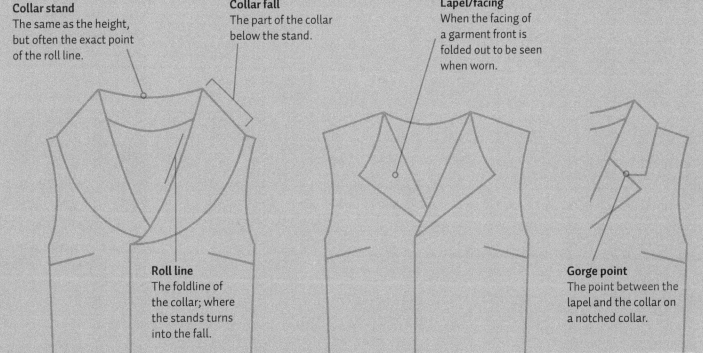

Collar stand
The same as the height, but often the exact point of the roll line.

Collar fall
The part of the collar below the stand.

Lapel/facing
When the facing of a garment front is folded out to be seen when worn.

Roll line
The foldline of the collar; where the stands turns into the fall.

Gorge point
The point between the lapel and the collar on a notched collar.

Flat Collar

The simplest collar to draft is a flat collar. It will work on any neckline. Flat collars are attached to the neckline and lie flat against the bodice. A flat collar can be any shape you dream up.

The flat collar drafting methods are the foundation for more complex collars. This collar goes best with a facing but can be sewn with a placket. Be sure to draft the placket or facing before drafting the collar. See the

facing or placket section for instructions.

Decide whether you want your collar to run all the way through the button extension or to meet at the center front. Most jackets

have a collar that extends through the button extension, allowing the collar to overlap at the center front. Blouses or base layers typically have collars that begin at the center front and do not overlap.

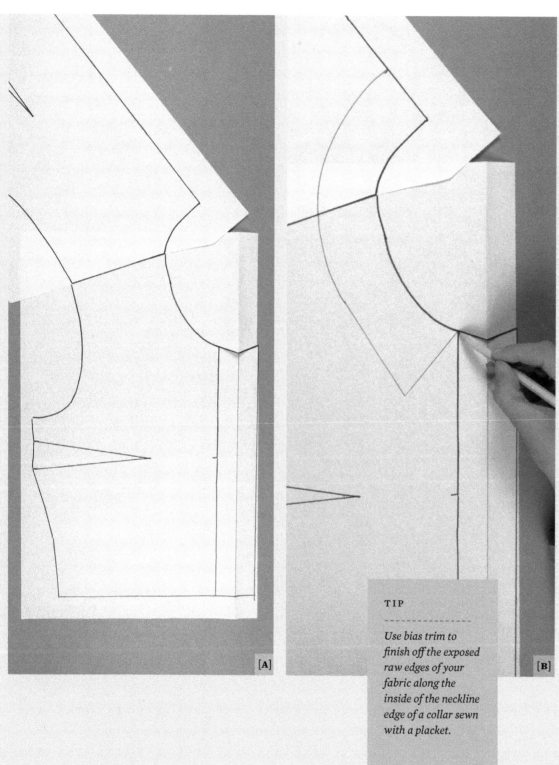

[A]

[B]

1
Draft your bodice, neckline, and the placket or facing first.

2
Position the front and back bodices together at the shoulder seams so that the neckline is in one continuous shape [**A**].

3
Draw the desired shape of your collar from the center front, or from the button extension foldline, to the center back. The back collar should be perpendicular to the center back bodice. This will allow the back collar to look like a shallow curve instead of having a point or scallop shape [**B**].

4
On a new piece of paper, trace the collar pattern piece. On the neckline edge of the collar, place a notch at the shoulder seam. This is the upper collar pattern piece. Place the grainline parallel to the center back [**C**].

TIP

- - - - - - - - - - - - - - -

Use bias trim to finish off the exposed raw edges of your fabric along the inside of the neckline edge of a collar sewn with a placket.

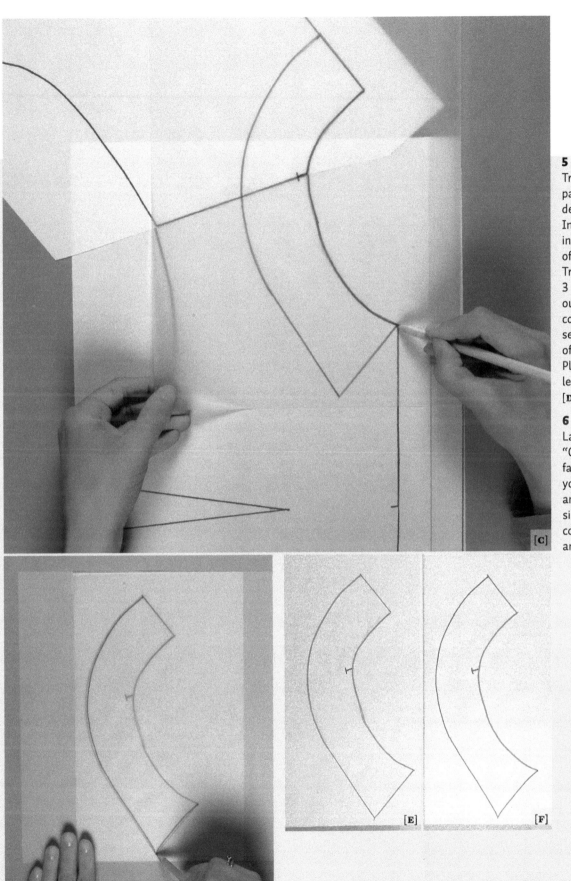

5
Trace the upper collar pattern to create the under collar pattern piece. Include the notch that indicates the placement of the shoulder seam. Trim ¹⁄₁₆" to ⅛" (2 to 3 mm) away from the outer edge of the under collar. This will hide the seam of the outer edge of the collar from view. Place the grainline parallel to the center back [D],[E],[F].

6
Label both collar patterns "Cut 1 on fold of self fabric." Depending on your fabric choice and the amount of structure desired, interface the under collar or both the upper and the under collar.

[C]

[D]

[E]

[F]

Standing Collar

Any collar that is not flat has a stand. A standing collar is attached to the bodice neckline, stands above it, and falls over the bodice, forming a tent-like shape. There are several styles of standing collars, including camp, notched, and shawl. Within each style is a wide array of shapes and sizes. Some collars are combined with lapels and some are simpler. Start with a simple collar and facing and later combine a lapel. Again, you can draft a standing collar to include a facing or placket.

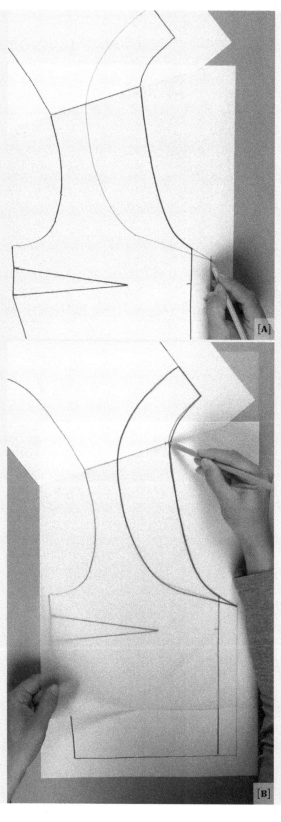

[A]

[B]

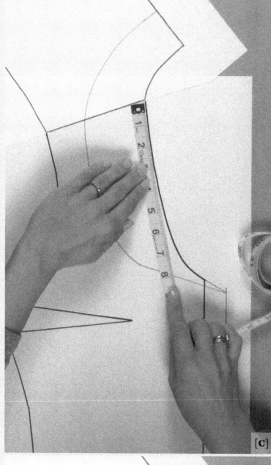

[C]

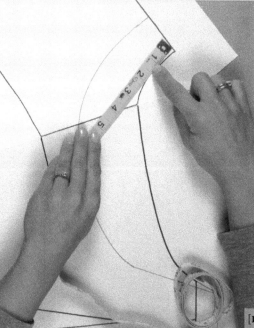

[D]

1
Draft your bodices, necklines, and facings or placket first.

Refer to photo [A] for steps 2 and 3.

2
Position the front and back bodices together at the shoulder seams so the neckline is in one continuous shape.

3
Draw the desired shape of your collar from the center front, or from the button extension foldline, to the center back. The back collar should be perpendicular to the center back bodice. This will allow the collar back to form a shallow curve instead of a point or scallop shape.

4
On a new piece of paper, trace the collar pattern piece. On the neckline edge of the collar, place a notch at the shoulder seam [B].

5
Measure and record your front neckline length from the center front or the button extension foldline to the shoulder [C]. Measure and record your back neckline length from the shoulder notch to the center back [D].

Add the two measurements together.

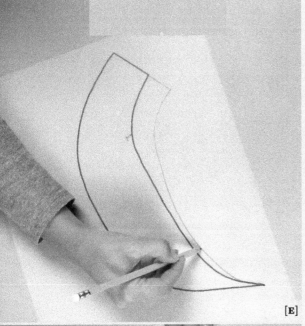

[E]

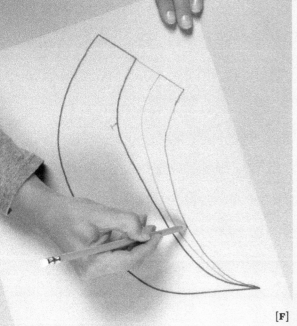

[F]

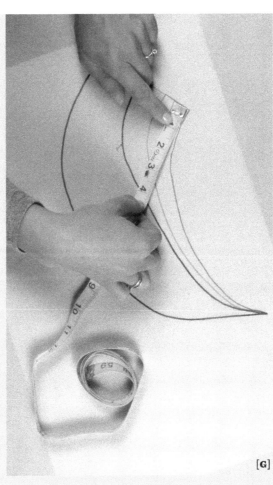

[G]

6

Decide on the stand of your collar, anywhere from ½" to 3" (1.3 to 7.6 cm).

Refer to photo [E] for steps 7 and 8.

7

On the collar pattern, extend the center back guideline above the back neckline by the desired height of your collar stand.

This line is your roll line, where the stand meets the fall of the collar.

8

Connect the extended center back to your original collar front, mimicking the original neckline shape. Make sure the roll line is perpendicular to the center back guideline for ½" (1.3 cm).

9

Repeat steps 7 and 8. This new line is the neck-line of your collar that gets sewn to the neckline of your bodice. For a collar with a larger stand, the neckline shape will be a very short curve [F].

10

Measure the new neck-line curve of the collar [G].

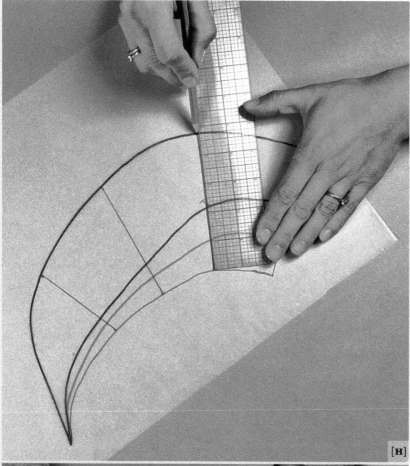

11

Subtract the new neckline curve from the original neckline measurements from step 5. Record the difference and divide by 3. Round your measurement to the nearest ⅛" or the nearest millimeter.

Refer to photo [H] for steps 12–14.

12

Divide the new neckline measurement by 5 and record the number. Starting from the center back guideline, measure one-fifth of the neckline edge and mark along the new neckline toward the front. Repeat twice so you have three marks on your neckline edge.

13

Measure and divide the outer collar edge by 5. Round your measurement to the nearest ⅛" or the nearest millimeter. Starting from the center back guideline, measure the amount calculated and mark along the outer collar edge toward the front. Repeat twice so you have three marks on your outer collar edge.

14

Connect the marks made on the neckline to the corresponding marks on the outer collar. These are your insertion lines. There should be only three insertions.

Refer to photo [I] for steps 15 and 16.

15

On each insertion line, cut from the neckline edge to the outer collar edge but not through it. Insert the amount determined in step 11.

16

Before securing the insertions with tape, measure the new neckline edge of the collar and adjust so it equals the bodice neckline measurement from step 5. If needed, adjust one or more insertions to create the correct neckline measurement.

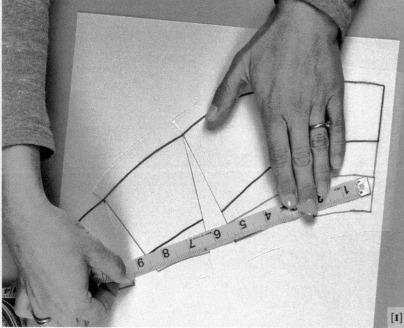

TIP

- - - - - - - - - - - - - - - - -

For collars and necklines, try using a ¼" (6 mm) seam allowance. It eliminates bulk and the need to trim seam allowances after sewing.

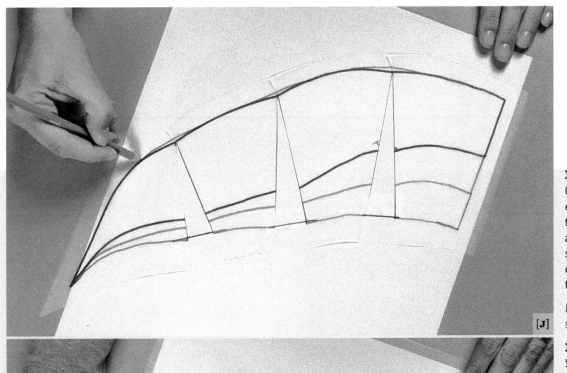

[J]

[K]

17
Connect the neckline edge of the collar across the insertions, creating a smooth curve. Do the same to the outer collar edge, especially where there are little dips [J].

Refer to photo [K] for steps 18–20.

18
Starting from collar break point, measure the distance recorded in step 5 along the neckline edge and notch to indicate your shoulder seam. Make sure the shoulder notch to the center back matches your back bodice neckline measurement. This is your upper collar.

19
Place the upper collar's grainline parallel to the center back guideline and label "Cut 1 on fold of self fabric."

20
Trace the upper collar pattern to create the under collar pattern piece.

Trim ¹⁄₁₆" to ⅛" (2 to 3 mm) away from the outer edge of the under collar. Place the grainline bias to the center back. Label "Cut 2 self and interfacing." Be sure to add seam allowance to the center back, as the center back will be sewn together [L].

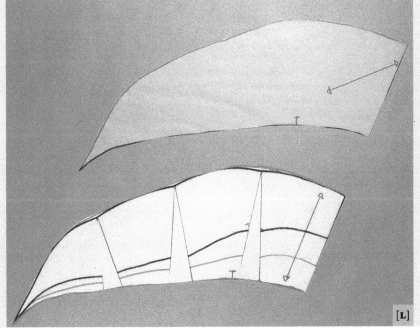

[L]

Adding a Lapel

A lapel is basically an exposed facing, a shaped portion of the center front and button extension that is folded to show on the outside of a finished garment. It is a great addition to a jacket. A lapel must be drafted on a V-neckline. A lapel can be added as the front neckline finish alone for a flap-style collar or be paired with a collar to create a notched collar. For a notched collar, a small part of the neckline may remain curved but the lapel portion must be drafted on a straight line.

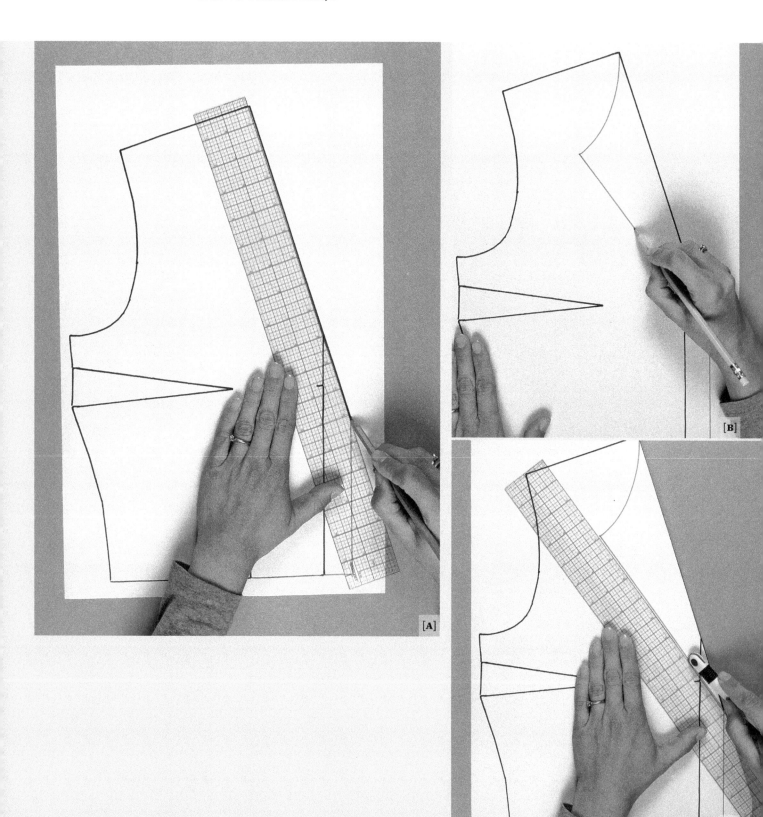

[A]

[B]

[C]

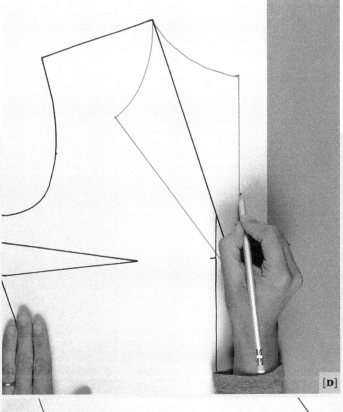

1

Draft your bodice with a V-neckline and button extension first. Do not draft the facing yet [**A**].

2

From your V-neckline edge, draw the shape of the lapel onto the bodice. The V-neckline becomes your roll line [**B**].

Refer to photo [C] for steps 3 and 4.

3

Fold your paper under at the roll line.

4

With a tracing wheel, trace the shape of the lapel onto drafting paper.

5

Unfold your paper and draw in the traced shape. It is fine if the lapel extends beyond the button extension and/or the center front guideline [**D**].

6

For a flap collar, continue by drafting a facing (see page 97). For a notched collar, proceed by following the standing collar instructions from page 102 and have the standing collar point meet up with the lapel drawn on the bodice front instead of the center front or the button extension [**E**].

[**D**]

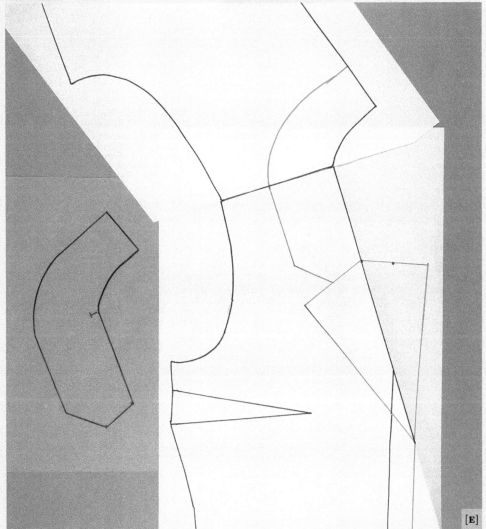

[**E**]

Collar with Band

A collar with band is the classic collar on a button-down shirt. A band replaces the collar's stand. The band gets sewn to the neckline and the collar gets sewn to the band. The band finishes off the raw edges of the neckline, eliminating the need for a facing, especially when combined with a placket. The collar fits best when it is on a natural or jewel neckline that sits close to the natural base of the neck.

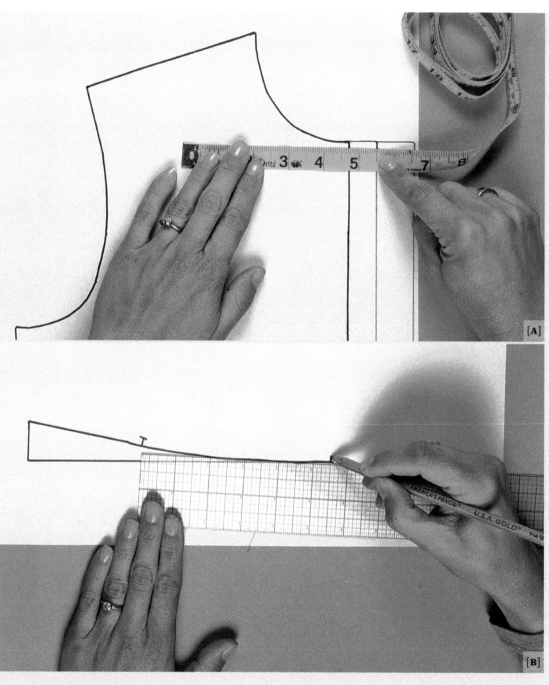

[A]

[B]

1
Draft a bodice with a placket.

2
Measure and record your front neckline measurement from the button extension foldline to the shoulder seam [A].

3
Measure and record the back neckline measurement from the shoulder to the center back.

4
Add the measurements together from steps 1 and 2. This is your band length.

Refer to photo [B] for steps 5–8.

5
Draw a horizontal line the length of your band measurement.

6
On the left side, draw a vertical line 1" (2.5 cm) up from the band measurement.

7
Draw a slight curve blending back to the right end of the band measurement line. This is your neckline of the band.

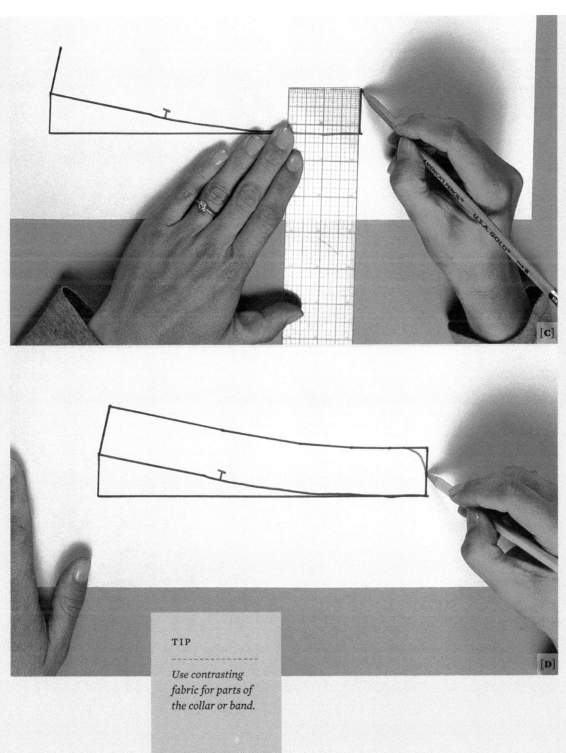

8

Measure along the curved line from the left your back neckline measurement. Mark the curved line with a notch.

9

Measure from the notch to the right of the front neckline measurement. Shorten or lengthen the line if needed.

10

Draw a line perpendicular to the neckline at the front and back that is the desired height of your band (¾" to 1½" [1.8 to 3.8 cm]). Connect these two points following the same curve of the neckline edge of the band [**C**].

11

If desired, curve the corner of the top of the band at the front [**D**].

[C]

[D]

TIP

Use contrasting fabric for parts of the collar or band.

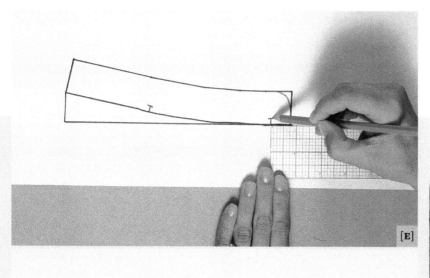

[E]

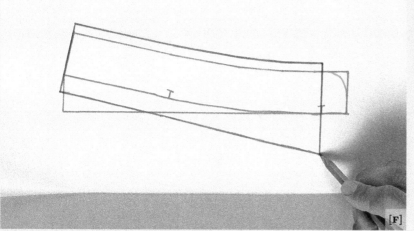

[F]

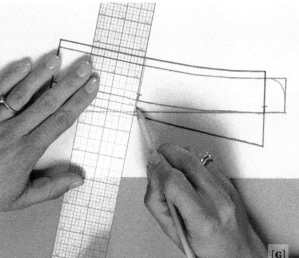

[G]

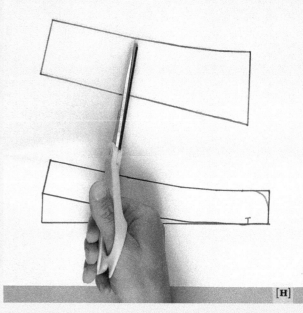

[H]

12

Measure and notch from the band's front edge toward the back at a point that is the width of the button extension from the bodice front. This is the center front notch [E].

13

On a new pattern paper, trace the shape of the band only to the notch, indicating the center front. Add ¼" to ½" (6 mm to 1.3 cm) to the top of the band. This will be the collar edge that gets sewn to the band.

Add ½" (1.3 cm) to the bottom of the band

until you reach the notch indicating the shoulder seam. From the shoulder seam toward the center front notch, continue to add ½" (1.3 cm) or more below. The more you add, the longer the collar points will be (think of a 1970s butterfly collar).

This is your collar pattern piece. Mark the shoulder notch [F].

14

Draw a vertical line across the collar pattern intersecting with the shoulder notch. This is an insertion line [G].

15

Cut from the outer collar edge to, but not through, the band edge [H]. Place paper behind the pattern and insert ⅜" (1 cm). Tape to secure. Connect the outer collar edge across the insertion. This is your upper collar pattern piece [I].

Adjust the shape of the collar: the closer the collar point is to center back, the wider the split will be in the collar at the center front.

The closer the collar is to the center front, the closer the collar points will be to meeting at the center front of the shirt.

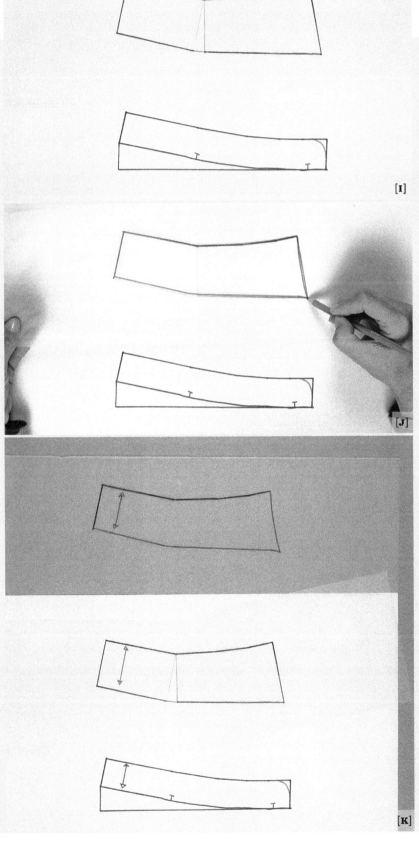

[I]

[J]

[K]

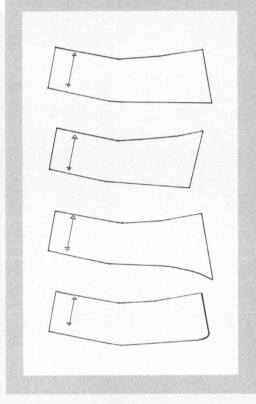

16
Trace the upper collar onto a new piece of paper and trim away ¹⁄₁₆" to ⅛" (2 to 3 mm) from the outer collar edge. Notice that the collar point does not get trimmed away. This is your under collar [J].

17
Place the grainline parallel to the center back on all pattern pieces: band, upper collar, and under collar. Label the band "Cut 2 on fold of self fabric" and "Cut 1 on fold of interfacing." [K]

Label the upper collar "Cut 1 on fold of self fabric."

Label the under collar "Cut 1 on fold of self fabric and interfacing."

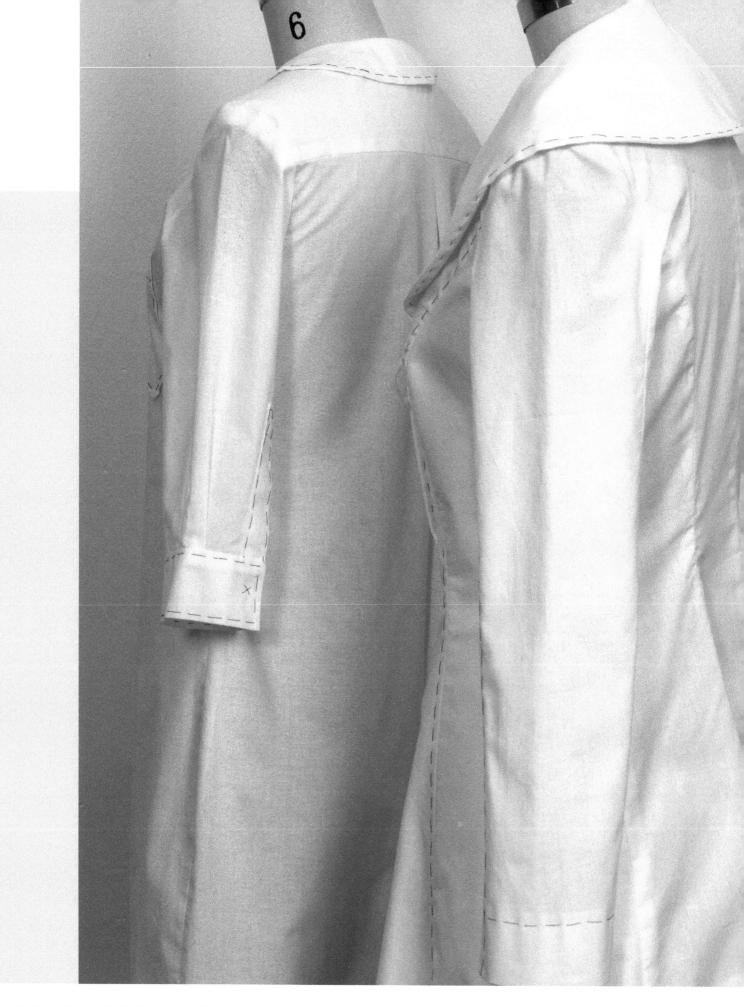

Sleeves

Just as with other portions of a garment, sleeves have many variations: short, long, blousy, tailored, full, cuffed, hemmed, or several of these elements combined. Sleeves and armholes go hand in hand, so if changes are made to the armhole, changes must be made to the sleeve. However, many style and silhouette changes can be made to the sleeve alone.

Unlike the armhole in a sleeveless garment that fits snugly to your body because of the armhole dart, the sleeved garment needs a more relaxed armhole. Review the section on Adding Ease (page 15) before designing sleeves.

In addition, the measurement of each sleeve cap should be larger than the measurement of its corresponding armhole on the garment's bodice. This is called ease. If the sleeve fits perfectly into the armhole measurement on a fitted garment, you cannot move your arm easily or with comfort.

Sleeve Guidelines

Back armhole notches
These are a set of double notches generally about 3" (7.6 cm) from the back underarm seam along the armhole curve.

Shoulder notch
This is the notch at the top of the sleeve cap that matches with the shoulder seam of the bodice front and back.

Bicep guideline
A horizontal guideline parallel to the base from the underarm seam front to the underarm seam back.

Front armhole notch
This is a notch generally about 3½" (8.9 cm) from the front underarm seam along the armhole curve.

Elbow guideline
A horizontal guideline parallel to the base roughly halfway down your underarm seam. While wearing your fitting shell, mark your elbow placement and transfer it to your paper pattern.

Quarter lines
Vertically oriented guidelines (though not perpendicular to the horizontal guidelines). These connect the base of your sleeve to your cap and will be instrumental in the drafting methods ahead. Follow instructions for finding your quarter lines.

Sleeve base measurement
A horizontal guideline at the base of your sleeve. This needs to be big enough for your hand to fit through for your master pattern.

To find your quarter lines, follow the steps below.

1
Divide the base into four equal parts and mark.

2
Connect the center base mark to the notch, indicating your shoulder seam. This is the center line.

3
Divide your bicep guideline into four parts and mark.

4
Connect the point from the back quarter base through the back quarter bicep to the cap of the sleeve.

5
Connect the point from the front quarter base through the front quarter bicep to the cap of the sleeve.

Shortening or Lengthening a Sleeve

This is the simplest way to change the character of your sleeve and is so easy to do. Use the horizontal guidelines to guide your adjustment.

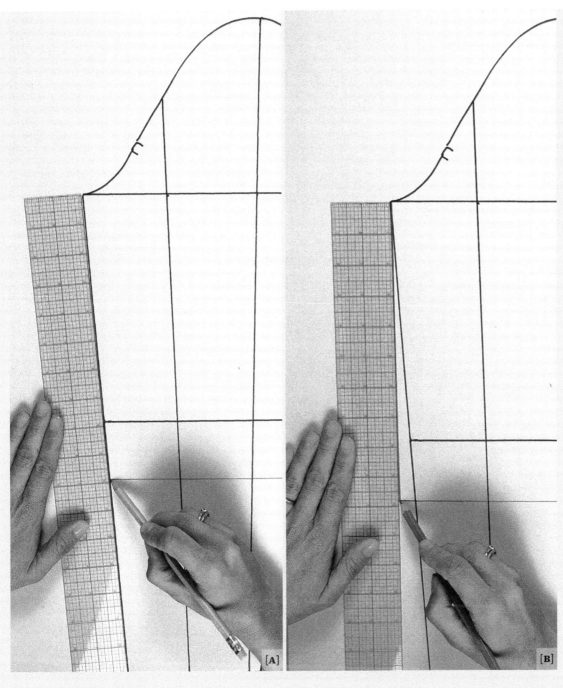

1
Decide on the new sleeve base. It should be parallel to one of your horizontal guidelines [A].

2
Measure the underarm seam length from the bicep guideline to the new base on the front and back to ensure they are the same length. Adjust the base as necessary [B].

Sleeve Ease

Calculate the differences between the sleeve's measurements and your body's measurements to determine the amount of ease in the sleeve. Keep your arm measurements and the amount of ease on each guideline for reference. The only measurement that will not be taken from your body is the armhole, as that is taken from your bodice patterns.

	Sleeve	−	Body/Bodice	=	Ease
Front sleeve cap / Front bodice armhole		−		=	
Back sleeve cap / Back bodice armhole		−		=	
Bicep		−		=	
Elbow		−		=	
Hand		−		=	
Wrist		−		=	

1
Measure around your bicep while your hand is on your shoulder.

2
Measure around your elbow while your hand is at your hip, slightly bent.

3
Measure around your wrist.

4
Measure around your hand as if you were about to take an oath, with your thumb alongside your palm.

TIP

- - - - - - - - - - - - - - -

Use a bias grainline on a sleeve without ease. Fabric that has nice bias give will not need the ease in the sleeve. To draw the new grainline, connect a new centerline and draw a line at a 45-degree angle to it. This is your bias grainline.

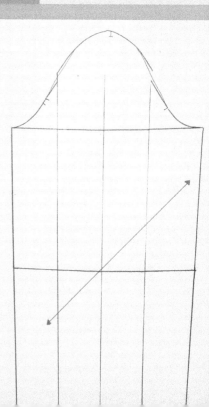

Removing Ease

Some sleeves do not need ease; these include a low cap, flared, gathered, pleated, or bias sleeve. These sleeves have added volume through the arm and ease can be removed from the cap, making the sleeve measurement match the armhole measurement. The ease will be removed from the quarter guidelines on your master sleeve pattern. Make a new master pattern of this sleeve if you like bias sleeves or sleeves with added volume.

TIP

Ease can be added to the sleeve pattern the same way. Instead of overlapping your sleeve on the quarter line, do insertions. These can be just at the cap or include the base, too.

[A]

[B]

[C]

[D]

1
Use the chart on the opposite page to determine the amount of ease in the sleeve cap on both the front and the back. The amount of ease may be different on the front versus the back.

2
Divide the amount of ease for the front by two. Note this calculation.

3
Divide the amount of ease for the back by two. Note this calculation.

4
Trace your basic sleeve pattern onto drafting paper.

5
On the front quarter line, cut from the cap to the base of the sleeve but not through it [A]. Overlap the cut by the amount calculated in step 2. Tape to secure [B].

6
On the back quarter line, cut from the cap to the base of the sleeve but not through it. Overlap the cut by the amount calculated in step 3. Tape to secure.

7
On the centerline, cut from the cap to the base of the sleeve but not through it. Overlap the cut by the amount calculated in step 2 plus step 3. Tape to secure.

8
Smooth out the shape of the sleeve cap by shaving off some of the sharp angles and filling in the shallow areas [C].

9
Measure from your back underarm seam toward the cap to the back armhole measurement. Notch to indicate the shoulder seam. Check to make sure your front sleeve measurement matches your front armhole measurement [D].

10
Continue to draft a new sleeve style or silhouette.

Low Cap Sleeve

Most fitting shells have a high cap sleeve that can restrict movement a bit. Lowering the cap provides a more relaxed fit. As you lower the cap, the bicep measurement becomes wider, thus making it more comfortable to wear. A high cap sleeve is most common on fitted women's garments, but the more relaxed the garment becomes, the better a low cap sleeve will work with your design. Men's shirts have sleeves with much lower caps.

Start with either a basic sleeve pattern or with a sleeve with ease removed.

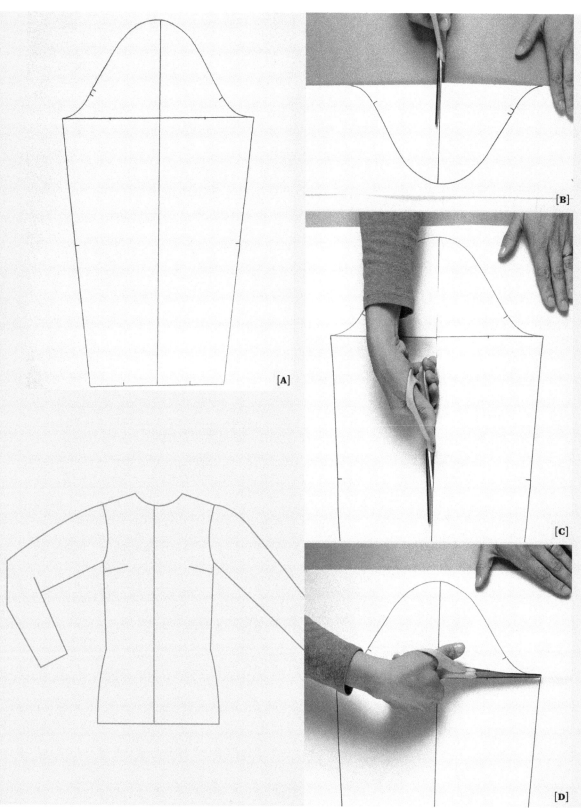

[A]

[B]

[C]

[D]

1
Trace your sleeve master pattern and mark the centerline and bicep guideline on the pattern [A].

2
Fold the paper in half on the bicep line and cut the centerline to create a hole [B]. Unfold the paper and continue cutting from the hole to the cap but not through it. Cut the hole to the base but not through it [C].

3
Cut the bicep line to both sides of the underarm seam but not through them. Trim the excess paper away from the perimeter to allow for pivoting [D].

If you prefer this low cap sleeve, make this a master pattern and draft other sleeve patterns from it. Sleeves with added fullness do not need to be drafted from a low cap sleeve because fullness will make the fit more comfortable.

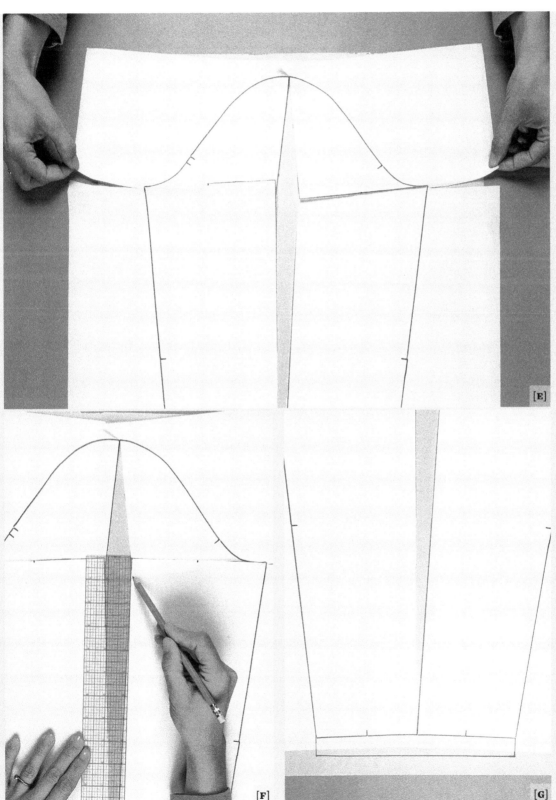

Refer to photo [E] for steps 4–6.

4
Place additional pattern paper underneath the sleeve.

5
Pull the underarm seams at the bicep guideline away from each other, lowering the cap. An opening forms vertically down the center while the bicep guideline begins to overlap.

6
Decide how much to lower your cap, ½" (1.3 cm) or more. Alternatively, you can decide how much additional width or ease you want on your bicep guideline.

[E]

7
Measure the amount of overlap that occurred at your bicep guideline and extend your sleeve this amount at the base to keep the overall length of your sleeve the same as the master pattern [F],[G].

[F]

[G]

Gathered Sleeve

A gathered sleeve can be very dramatic and add fullness from the cap to the hem, or have just a little hint of fullness at the cap or hem. Oftentimes a gathered sleeve is tapered at the base or has a gathered base that is sewn to a band or cuff.

A gathered sleeve can start from any master pattern, but the high cap sleeve with or without ease works very well. You will have a few drafting options in the instructions following. Experiment!

TIP

Before inserting volume, add a band or cuff. See page 124, Bands and Cuffs, for instructions.

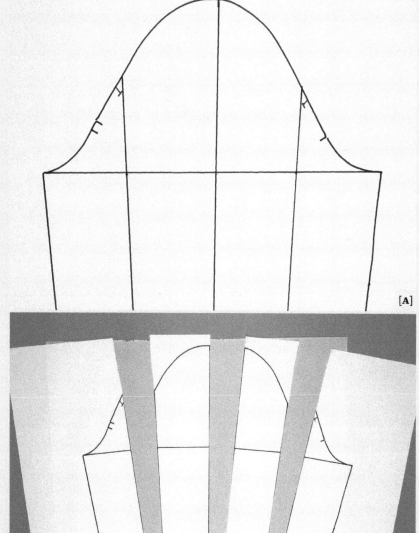

[A]

[B]

1
Trace the chosen sleeve master pattern onto drafting paper.

2
Determine the length of the sleeve.

3
Decide where you want the fullness in your sleeve design. It can be all across the sleeve cap or just 1" (2.5 cm) to each side of your shoulder notch. Notch this distance on your sleeve and on your bodice [A].

Refer to photos [B] and [C] for steps 4–8.

4
Draw insertion lines between your notches from the cap to the base of the sleeve. If your notches are only 2" (5.1 cm) apart, then one insertion line is sufficient. If you are gathering the whole cap of your sleeve, use your quarter lines as insertion lines.

5
Cut from the cap down to the base. If you want only the cap gathered, then add fullness to the cap. If you want fullness from the cap all the way to the hem or gathered to a band, then cut your insertions lines all the way through the base of the sleeve. To keep work manageable, cut only one insertion line at a time.

6
Place paper behind the insertion lines. For a sleeve with fullness to the base, draw a horizontal line on this paper. Place the sleeve base level with this line. Secure with tape.

TIP

To allow the gathered sleeve to puff above your shoulder, instead of fall off it, shave ½" to 1" (1.3 to 2.5 cm) off of your armhole at the shoulder seam on the bodice front and back. Blend the armhole back to its original shape at the cross front and cross back guidelines.

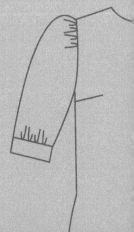

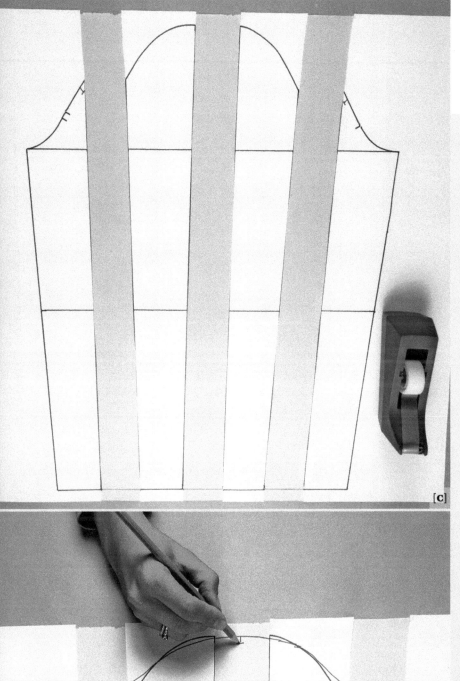

[C]

[D]

TIP

Add extra length to your sleeve and gather the base to your wrist measurement with a fitted cuff or an elasticized facing for a sleeve that blouses or balloons over your hand.

7
Measure over from the first pattern section the amount of volume desired, 1" to 3" (2.5 to 7.6 cm). Place the next sleeve section at the measured distance and secure in place with tape.

8
Repeat for all remaining insertion lines.

9
The base should be a smooth line; however, the cap will look very uneven [**C**]. Thoroughly smooth out sharp angles and fill in any shallow areas across insertion lines [**D**]. The new sleeve shape should maintain the original shape from the master pattern between the underarm seam and the front and back armhole notches.

10
Maintain the grainline from the sleeve master pattern. Label the pattern "Cut 2 of self fabric."

Flare

Adding flare or fullness to a sleeve is accomplished the same way as on a skirt. On a sleeve with flare from the cap, remove the ease from the cap first. A sleeve with flare added on a style-line below your bicep guideline should maintain the ease from your basic sleeve pattern.

TIP

Before inserting volume, add a band or cuff. See page 124 for instructions.

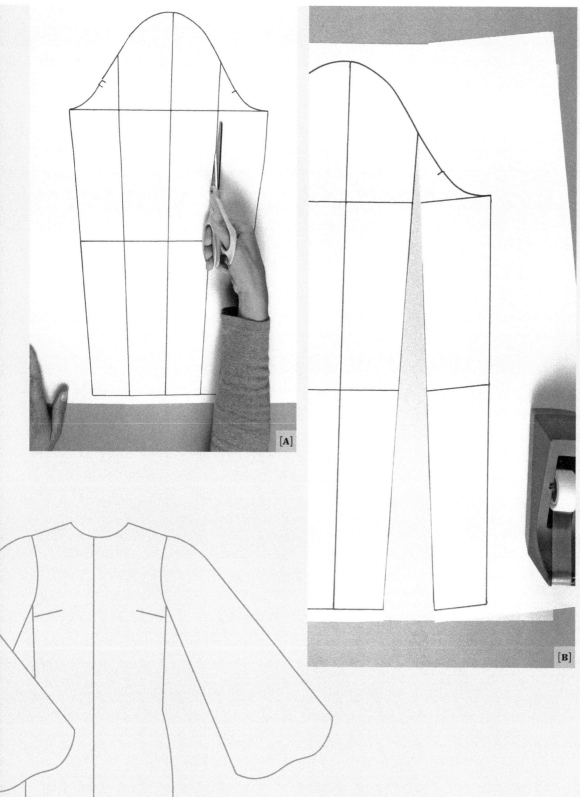

[A]

[B]

1

Trace your master sleeve pattern without ease onto drafting paper.

2

Adjust the length of the sleeve.

3

Mark the quarter lines on your draft. These are your insertion lines. Add more insertion lines if you want a very full sleeve [A].

Refer to photo [B] for steps 4 and 5.

4

Cut from the base to the cap but not through it. To keep work manageable, cut only one insertion line at a time.

5

Insert ½" to 2" (1.3 to 5.1 cm) at the base. If you want more volume, add more insertion lines between the front and back quarter lines.

Do not add more volume to the underarm portion of the sleeve.

TIP

Gather or pleat the excess volume to a cuff or an elastic casing, bringing the base measurement back to your hand or wrist measurement.

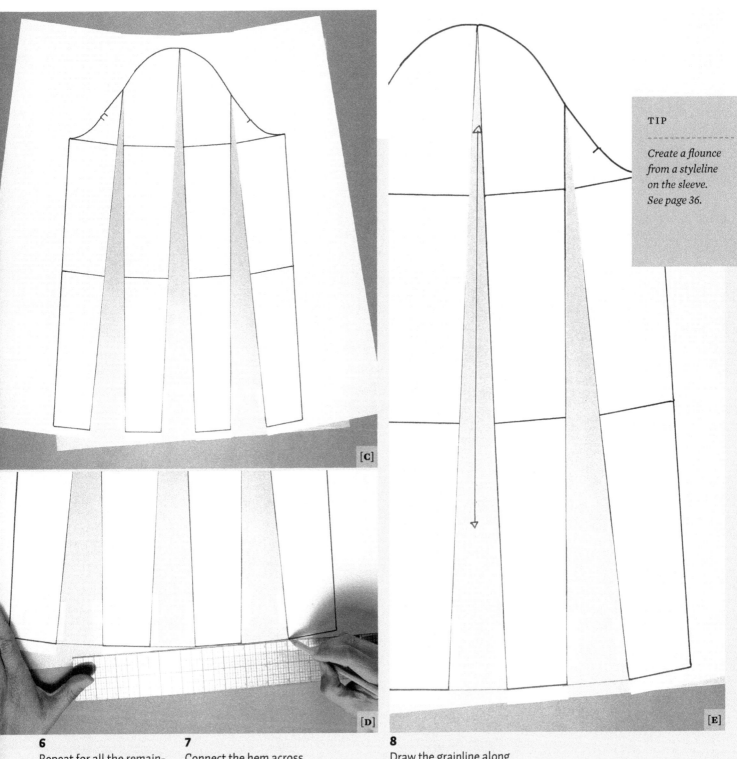

[C]

[D]

[E]

TIP

Create a flounce from a styleline on the sleeve. See page 36.

6
Repeat for all the remaining quarter and insertion lines. All insertion amounts should be equal [C].

7
Connect the hem across the insertions.

Smooth out any points by slightly curving the line, if necessary [D].

8
Draw the grainline along the centerline of the sleeve pattern. You may need to measure to find the new centerline at the base of the sleeve. Label your pattern "Cut 2 of self fabric" [E].

Bands and Cuffs

Bands and cuffs are a way to finish off the base of your sleeve. A band is sewn all the way around the sleeve base with no opening. A cuff is paired with a slit or a placket and can be unbuttoned. A band has to be at least as big as the hand measurement. A cuff can have a measurement smaller than the hand because it can be unbuttoned to make it larger. Start with the band instructions and then continue if you want to draft a cuff.

Band

Bands are a very simple way to finish off the base of a sleeve or even the base of a skirt or pant. Because the band pattern and function is simpler than a cuff it is less fussy to sew, however, it has the same impact as a cuff.

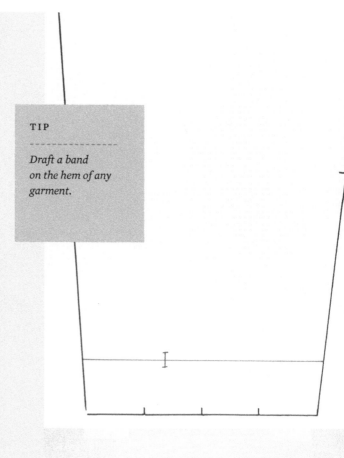

TIP

- - - - - - - - - - - - - - - -

Draft a band on the hem of any garment.

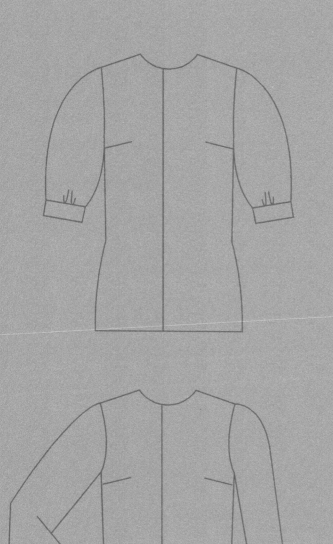

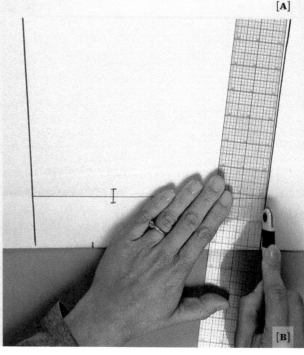

[A]

[B]

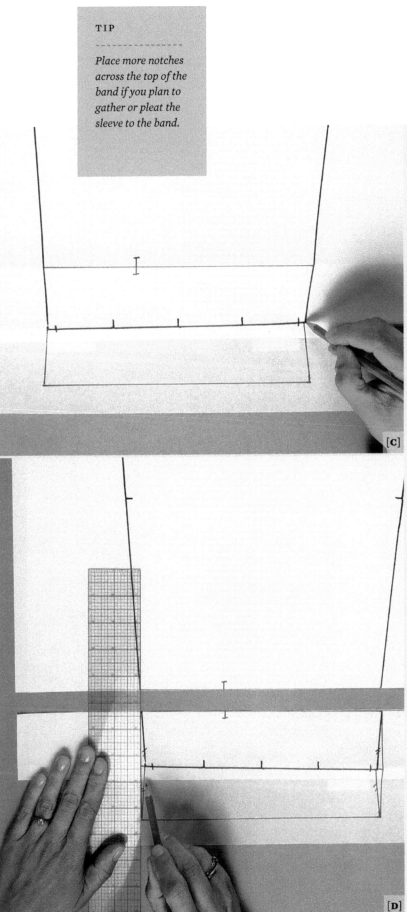

TIP

- - - - - - - - - - - - - - - - -

Place more notches across the top of the band if you plan to gather or pleat the sleeve to the band.

1
Trace your chosen sleeve master pattern onto drafting paper.

2
Decide on the finished length of your sleeve, including the band.

Refer to photo [A] for steps 3 and 4.

3
Draw a horizontal line parallel to your base the desired height of your band.

4
Place a notch across this line.

5
Fold the paper pattern under on the sleeve base and trace the underarm seam and the top of the band with a tracing wheel [B]. Unfold, draw the traced shape, and notch on the foldline. This is your band pattern piece [C].

6
Cut the band pattern away from the sleeve pattern [D].

7
Draw any grainline you choose for the band. Label the pattern "Cut 2 of self fabric and interfacing."

8
Continue to draft the sleeve as desired.

[C]

TIP

- - - - - - - - - - - - - - - - -

Remove the original underarm seam shaping and create a rectangular band. This works great on a band that is 3" (7.6 cm) or shorter in height.

[D]

Cuff

A cuffed sleeve allows for the sleeve to be more fitted around the base because you can unbutton the cuff to allow your hand to pass through. A cuff can be your wrist measurement with ease, making it smaller than your hand. If you want a more traditional button-front shirt sleeve, where you can roll your cuff up over your elbow, you will not want to adjust the base of your sleeve. Cuffs can be as short as ¾ inch (1.8 cm) or as tall as you like. The taller the cuff, the more shaping it needs to have to fit over the forearm properly.

1
Follow steps 1–3 for the band.

2
Adjust the base of the sleeve, if desired. Bring in the base on each side equally to make the cuff to your wrist measurement plus ease. Connect the new base width to the underarm seam on the bicep guideline [A].

3
Fold the paper pattern under on the sleeve base and trace the underarm seam and the top of the cuff with a tracing wheel. Unfold and draw the traced shape [B].

TIP

Remove the original underarm seam shaping and create a rectangular cuff. This works great on a cuff that is 3" (7.6 cm) or shorter in height.

[A]

[B]

TIP

Buttons on cuffs and plackets are typically 5⁄8″ (1.5 cm) or less.

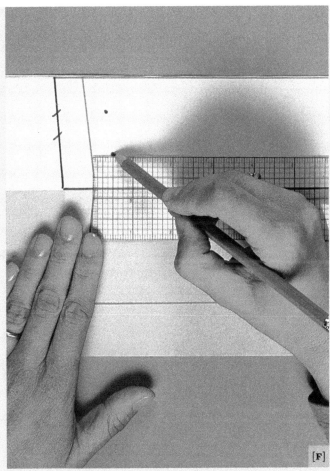

[F]

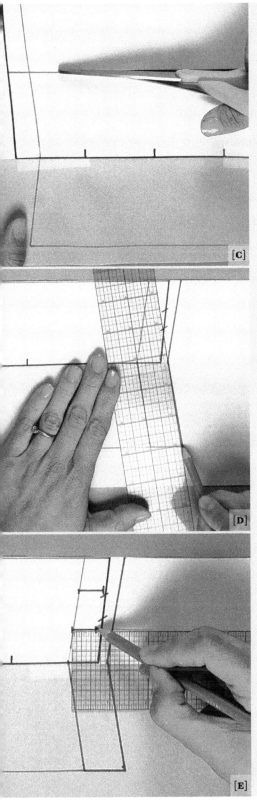

[C]

[D]

[E]

4

Cut your cuff pattern away from the base of the sleeve [C].

5

Add 1″ (2.5 cm) to one side of your cuff. This is the buttonhole extension side [D].

6

Position one or more horizontal buttonholes 3⁄8″ (1 cm) from the edge of the cuff. Make the buttonhole 1⁄8″ (3 mm) bigger than the button diameter. The position of the buttonholes can be centered or spaced as desired [E].

7

Mark the button position with an awl punch 1⁄2″ (1.3 cm) from the button edge at the same level as the buttonhole [F].

8

Draw any grainline you choose for the cuff. Label the pattern "Cut 2 of self fabric and interfacing."

9

Draft your sleeve with cuff.

Sleeve with Cuff

The base of the sleeve will be pleated or gathered to the cuff. The sleeve will have a placket because when the cuff opens and closes, the sleeve has to as well. The sleeve and the cuff open near the back quarter line of the sleeve. A sleeve is always bigger than the cuff by at least 2 inches (5.1 cm); this allows for two small pleats or light gathers, though the sleeve can be much fuller than the cuff by patterning flare or gathers.

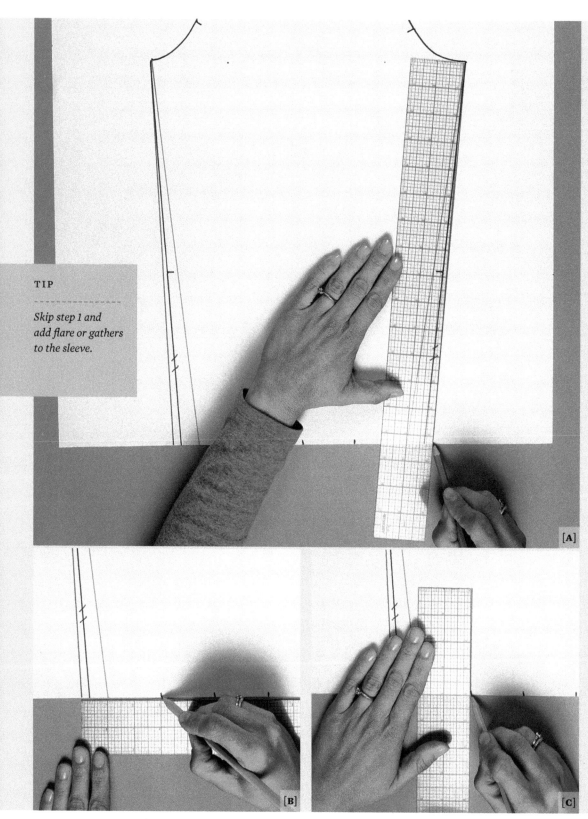

TIP

Skip step 1 and add flare or gathers to the sleeve.

[A]

[B]

[C]

1
Extend the base of each underarm seam at least 1" (2.5 cm). Connect the extension to the bicep guideline on the underarm seam [**A**].

2
Along the base, measure 3" (7.6 cm) from the back underarm seam. This is the slit or placket position [**B**].

3
Draw a line perpendicular to the base and up the height of your desired placket opening, 3" (7.6 cm) or more. Mark the top with an awl punch and the base with a notch [**C**].

This is your cut line.

TIP

Add extra length to the sleeve so that it will blouse over the cuff at the wrist. Use your elbow guideline as an insertion line and add 2" (5.1 cm) or more length.

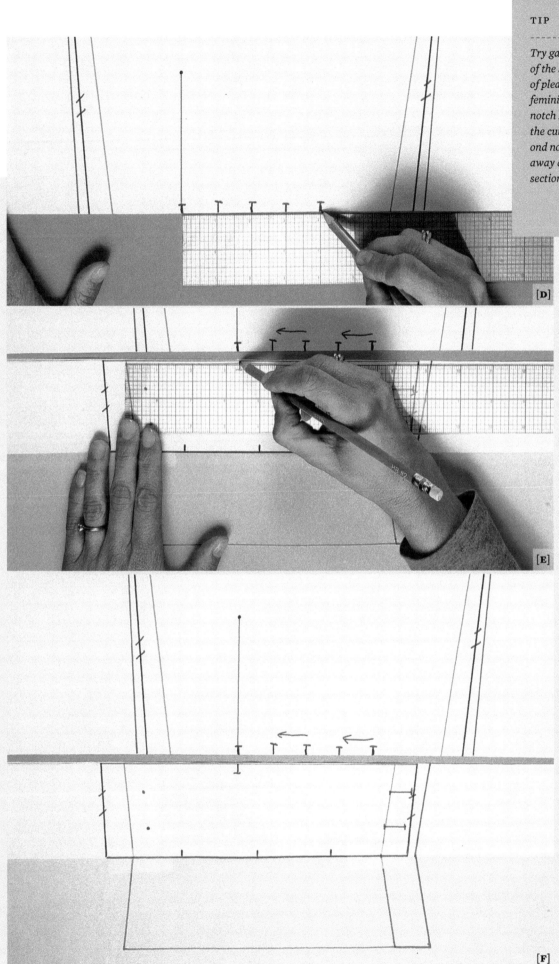

TIP
----
*Try gathering the base
of the sleeve instead
of pleating for a more
feminine look. Place a
notch 1" (2.5 cm) from
the cut line and a sec-
ond notch 4" (10.2 cm)
away and gather the
section to 2" (5.1 cm).*

[D]

[E]

4
Starting 1" (2.5 cm) from
your cut line toward the
front of the sleeve, draw
four notches 1" (2.5 cm)
apart. The first two will
create one pleat, there
will be 1" (2.5 cm) space
between, and the last
two notches will create
the second pleat. These
pleats take up the extra
volume you added to
the sides of the sleeve
in step 1 [D].

5
Measure the distance
from your underarm seam
to the cut line, add ⅜"
(1 cm), and from the
button side of your cuff
mark this distance with a
notch. The button side is
opposite the buttonhole
side with the 1" (2.5 cm)
extension [E],[F].

6
Maintain the original
grainline of your sleeve
master pattern. Label
the pattern "Cut 2 of
self fabric."

7
Draft your placket.

[F]

Sleeve Placket

A sleeve placket allows for a finished slit on the sleeve just above the cuff opening. They are 1 inch (2.5 cm) wide and can be 3 inches (7.6 cm) or greater in length. A smaller placket may not have any buttons on it, but a longer one could have two or more buttons. The buttons are typically ½ to ⅝ inch (1.3 to 1.5 cm) and the buttonholes are vertical. The top of a placket can be any shape—square, angled, or house shaped. This small area allows for your own creativity.

TIP

Place a placket down from a neckline on a shirt front. Just mark your cut line right down the center front guideline and draft the placket the same way as instructed.

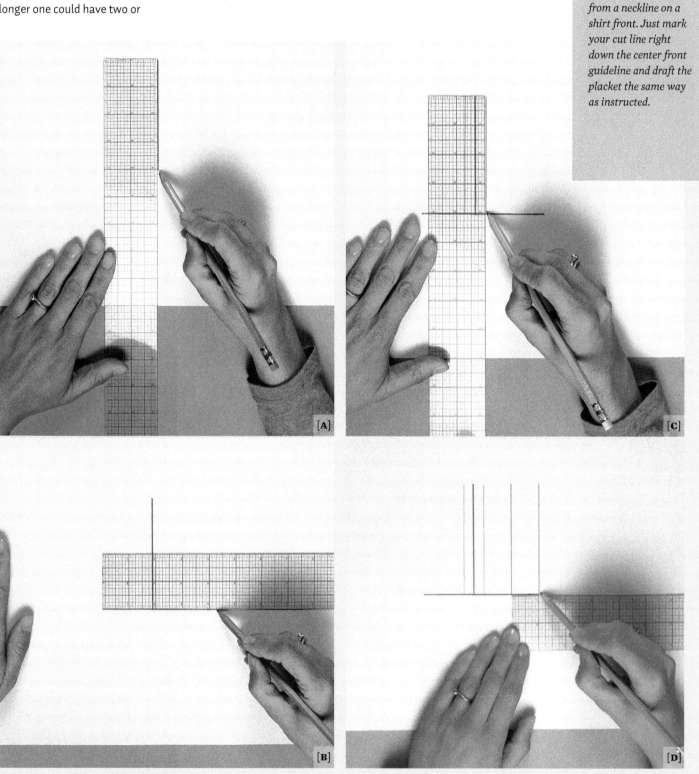

1
Draw a line the same length as the cut mark on the sleeve from the Sleeve with Cuff instructions step 3. This is the cut line of your placket [**A**].

2
Draw a perpendicular line to the bottom 1⅞" (4.8 cm) to the left and 2⅜" (6.1 cm) to the right [**B**].

3
From your cut line measure over ⅜" (1 cm) to the left and right and draw a line parallel to the cut line. These are the sewing lines [**C**].

*Refer to photo [**D**] for steps 4 and 5.*

4
Measure 1" (2.5 cm) to the right side of your sewing line and draw a line parallel to it. Notch at the base; this is a foldline.

5
Measure an additional 1" (2.5 cm) from your right foldline and draw a line parallel to it. This is the edge of your placket pattern.

[**E**]

[**F**]

[**G**]

*Refer to photo [**E**] for steps 6 and 7.*

6
Measure ¾" (1.8 cm) to the left side of your sewing line and draw a line parallel to it. Notch at the top and base; this is a foldline.

7
Measure an additional ¾" (1.8 cm) to the left side of your foldline and draw a line parallel to it. This is the edge of your placket.

*Refer to photos [**F**] and [**G**] for steps 8 and 9.*

8
On the right side, extend the top of the placket up at least 1" (2.5 cm). Make it whatever shape you want above the 1" (2.5 cm).

9
Draw a horizontal line at the top to connect the left side of the placket to the tower on the right.

10
Mark the grainline parallel to the cut line.

Label the pattern piece "Cut 2 self fabric and interfacing."

TIP

- - - - - - - - - - - - - - -

The placket is easier to sew with only ¼" (6 mm) seam allowance on all sides, excluding the base.

Two-Piece Sleeve

There are a number of seamlines you can create to make a sleeve with two pattern pieces. The most conventional two-piece sleeve has vertical seams at the quarter lines, eliminating the underarm seam. Another variation maintains the underarm seam and adds a seam on the centerline of the sleeve. Each has different benefits that accompany the additional seams. Quarter line seams can shape the sleeve with a forward bend that mimics the natural bend of a relaxed arm. A sleeve with a centerline seam eliminates the ease in the sleeve because it can be shaped at the cap. This sleeve can also be set very high on the shoulder as opposed to just off the edge of it. Try out these traditional two-piece sleeves and then create unique styleline combinations of your own design.

Quarter Line Two-Piece Sleeve

A shaped two-piece sleeve generally falls on or near your quarter lines because these lines are very close to the front and back bend of your arm. You can really place them anywhere you want. Try drafting a two-piece sleeve on these lines first and then alter the seam position for later designs. A high cap master sleeve pattern is a good one to start with.

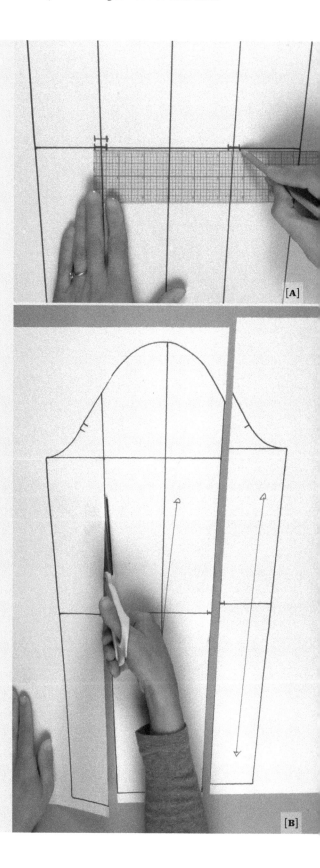

1

Trace your high cap master sleeve pattern onto drafting paper. Make any changes to the length and style first.

2

Draw your quarter lines on the pattern. These will be your stylelines.

3

Place a double notch across the quarter line at the elbow guideline on the back of the sleeve. Place a single notch across the quarter line of the front sleeve [A].

Refer to photo [B] for steps 4 and 5.

4

Place your grainline on the sleeve, both in the center and on the front quarter, before separating the pattern.

5

Cut the sleeve on the quarter lines.

TIP

Change the position of the seam more to your liking after testing the basic quarter line style first.

TIP

Add a vent on the back seam of the sleeve. See page 170 for instructions.

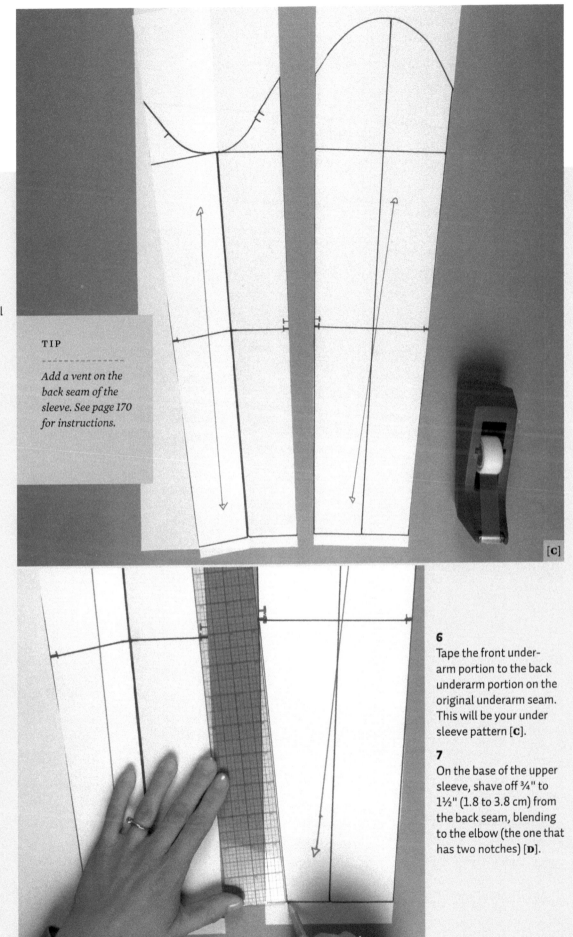

[C]

[D]

6

Tape the front underarm portion to the back underarm portion on the original underarm seam. This will be your under sleeve pattern [C].

7

On the base of the upper sleeve, shave off ¾" to 1½" (1.8 to 3.8 cm) from the back seam, blending to the elbow (the one that has two notches) [D].

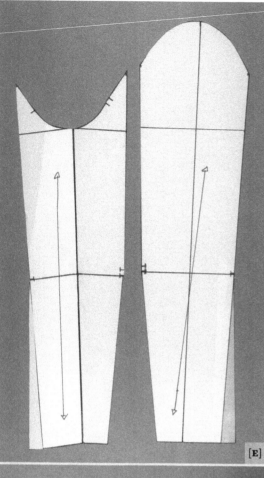

[E]

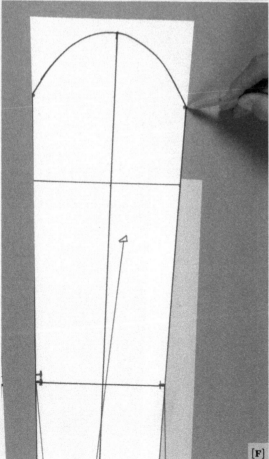

[F]

Refer to photo [E] for steps 8 and 9.

8
On the base of the upper sleeve, extend ¾" to 1½" (1.8 to 3.8 cm) to the front seam, blending to the elbow.

9
Repeat steps 6 and 7 for the underarm sleeve.

10
Awl punch the sleeve cap at each front and back seam on both the upper and the under sleeve patterns [F].

11
Label the pieces "Cut 2 of self fabric."

Centerline Two-Piece Sleeve

The two-piece sleeve on the centerline is great with a fitted jacket and a narrow shoulder seam because the sleeve can be shaped to the curve of your shoulder.

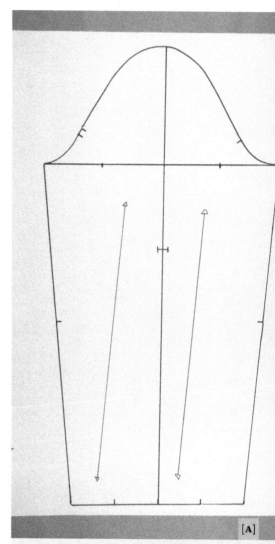

[A]

1
Trace your high cap master sleeve pattern onto drafting paper. Make any changes to length and style first.

Refer to photo [A] for steps 2 and 3.

2
Draw in your centerline from the shoulder notch to the sleeve base. This is your styleline.

TIP

- -

Cut away a portion of your bodice from the notches in the armhole to the shoulder seam and tape this to your sleeve cap, overlapping the curves slightly to create a raglan-styled sleeve.

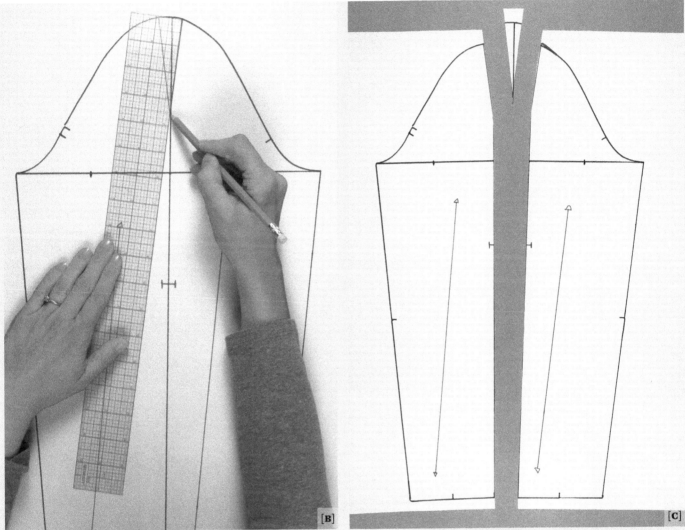

[B]

[C]

3
Draw in your grainline on both the front and the back sleeve sections. Notch the center styleline between the cap and elbow guideline.

Refer to photo [B] for steps 4–6.

4
Using the chart from the beginning of this section to determine ease (see page 116), shave off the ease from back sleeve cap, blending into the styleline with a soft curve at least 2" (5.1 cm) above your bicep guideline.

5
Shave off the amount of front ease from the front sleeve cap, blending into the styleline at least 2" (5.1 cm) above your bicep guideline.

6
Measure the seam length of the centerline on both the front and the back between the cap and the bicep guideline. If they are not equal, raise the cap of the shorter length if the difference is ¼" (6 mm) or less. If the difference is greater than ¼" (6 mm), then adjust both the front and the back to make the seam length equal.

7
Cut the pattern apart on the styleline from the base to the cap and discard the darted ease [C].

8
Label each piece "Cut 2 of self fabric."

Pants

Many commercial pattern companies make a simple pant pattern that can be modified to create multiple styles.

———

As with shopping off the rack, finding a good-fitting pant pattern can also be a challenge. It may take you several fittings before you arrive at a happy place.

———

If using a commercial pattern, spend time with the fit first; it will be worthwhile in the long run. The best pant silhouette to start working with is your favorite.

The Master Pant Pattern Library

Pant Variations

Unlike a simple skirt master pattern that can supply endless silhouette changes with good success, pant master patterns fall into three categories, similar to bodices: fitted, relaxed, and relaxed with a full leg. The more relaxed a pant rise and leg are, the easier it is to fit. As the pant leg becomes more tapered and fitted, more time will need to be spent on fitting.

Testing fit on new styles is imperative, and I encourage you to use a fabric that is similar to your final fashion fabric. If you are designing stretch, find inexpensive stretch denim with properties similar to the final fabric to test the fit.

You may already have one or more favorite pant silhouettes with a pattern that works for you. Now you can make them master pant patterns. Eliminate all pocket, zipper, and yoke details so you can design new elements with more freedom.

Guidelines

It is important to know how much ease you have on each guideline, especially if you want to pattern a pant with a fitted leg. See Measurements on page 13.

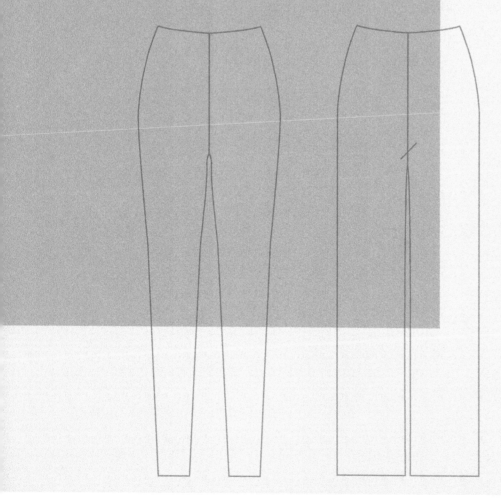

Hip level

A horizontal guideline at the fullest point below the waist perpendicular to the grainline and connecting the center to the side seam. It is often marked on commercial patterns, but make sure it is where you are fullest; it may be higher or lower.

Crotch level

A horizontal guideline parallel to the base and perpendicular to the grainline that connects the crotch point to the side seam. The **crotch point** is where the inseam meets the rise of the pant. The crotch-level guideline on a pant front will not match the crotch level guideline on the side seam.

Knee

A horizontal guideline parallel to the base and perpendicular to the grainline at the level of your knee. This is easiest to mark while wearing a fitting shell.

Calf

A horizontal guideline parallel to the base and perpendicular to the grainline about 5" (12.7 cm) below your knee. This is easiest to mark while wearing a fitting shell.

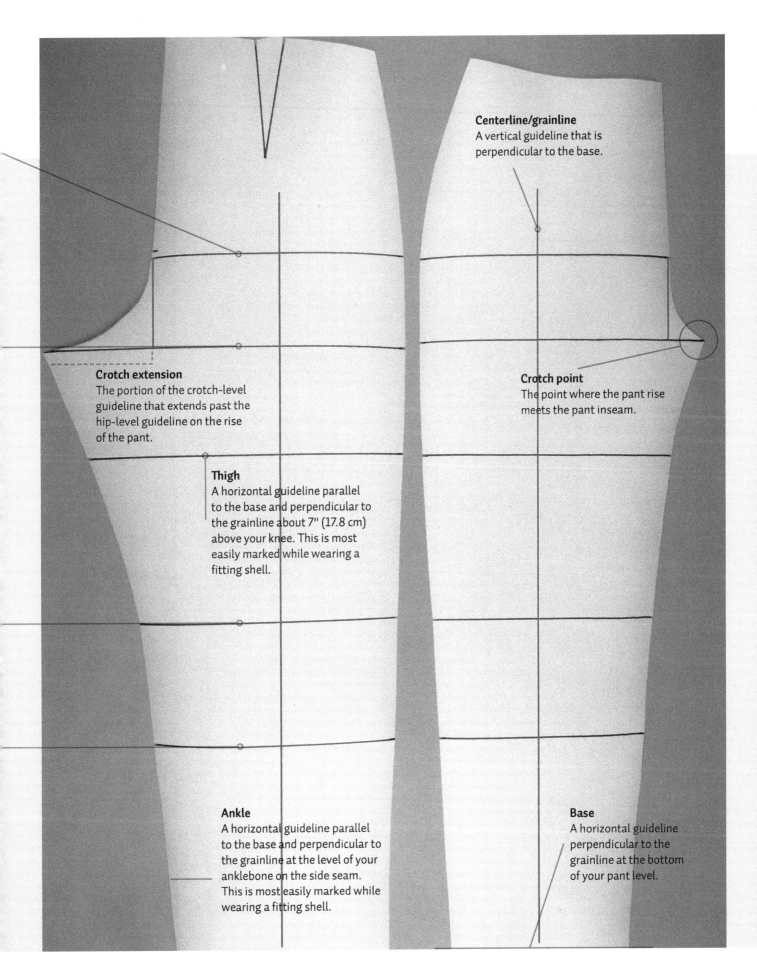

Centerline/grainline
A vertical guideline that is perpendicular to the base.

Crotch extension
The portion of the crotch-level guideline that extends past the hip-level guideline on the rise of the pant.

Crotch point
The point where the pant rise meets the pant inseam.

Thigh
A horizontal guideline parallel to the base and perpendicular to the grainline about 7" (17.8 cm) above your knee. This is most easily marked while wearing a fitting shell.

Ankle
A horizontal guideline parallel to the base and perpendicular to the grainline at the level of your anklebone on the side seam. This is most easily marked while wearing a fitting shell.

Base
A horizontal guideline perpendicular to the grainline at the bottom of your pant level.

Making a Master Pant Pattern

Most master pant patterns that you create should be cleared of design details so that you can design more freely and without obstacles. You may want to change the waistline, waist finish, shape of the pocket opening and bags, where the closure is, and more. Pockets are the easiest to eliminate by laying the pattern pieces on top of one another and then tracing the full pattern perimeter. However, yokes and waistbands can be more challenging to reverse engineer. It can be helpful to read through the instructions on pages 24–33 in the Skirts chapter for how to draft these elements in the first place before trying to undo them.

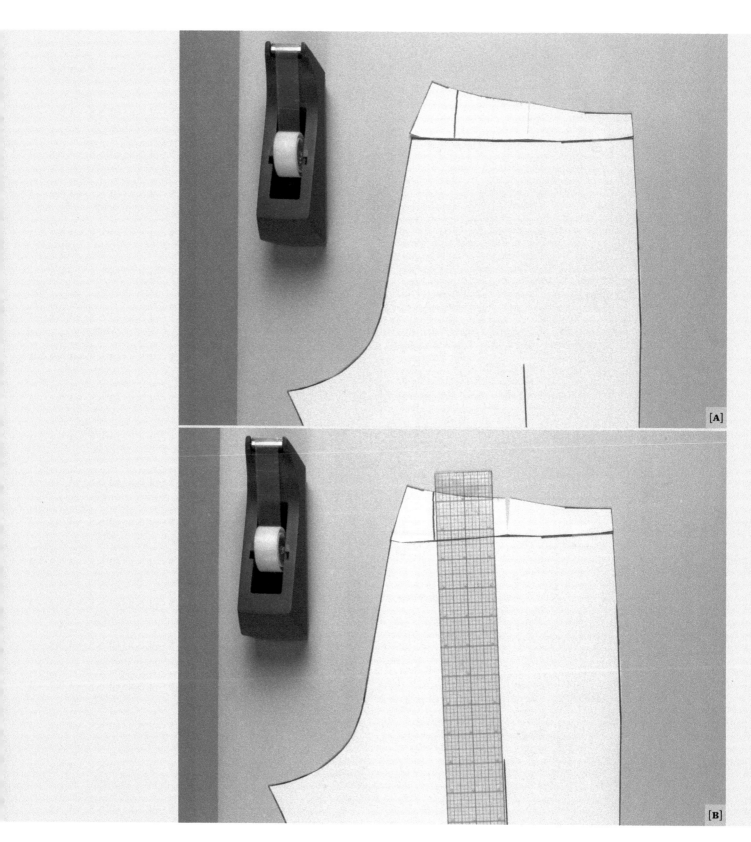

[A]

[B]

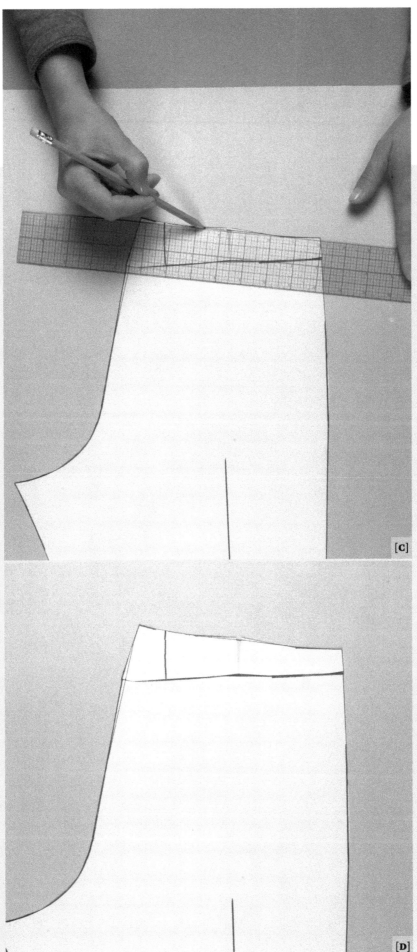

Refer to photo [A] for steps 1–4.

1
Copy your pant master pattern onto drafting paper, excluding seam allowance. Include the grainline.

2
Copy your waistline finish onto another sheet of drafting paper, excluding seam allowance, and cut the pattern out.

3
Align the center back of the waistline finish to the pant center back. The seamline between the pant waist and the base of the waistline finish should be aligned for a few inches.

4
Cut from the top of the waistline finish to the base, but not through it, where the waistline finish curves away from the pant.

This should be about midway through the back waist measurement.

Refer to photo [B] for steps 5 and 6.

5
Spread the waistline finish apart so the remaining portion of it lies in line with the pant and the grainline on the pant aligns with the grainline of the waist finish or yoke. There may be a little overlap.

6
Place drafting paper behind the opening. Tape to secure and mark this as a dart.

7
Smooth out any sharp angles or dips where the pattern pieces join [C],[D].

8
Repeat steps 1–7 for the front pant pattern.

[C]

[D]

Changes to a Fitted Pant

A pant is made more fitted with simple pattern changes that create a dramatic difference. Even though the drafting is straightforward, more time should be spent on making a muslin and fitting.

It may seem like a bit of work to get the fit right; remember that this becomes a master pattern and can be used a thousand times over.

ADJUSTMENTS TO A PANT SILHOUETTE

Adjustments can be made to any pant pattern to create another style master pattern. Changing the extension on the crotch-level guideline and the shaping through the leg will dramatically alter the fit.

Regardless of the change in silhouette, the ratio of the front crotch extension needs to maintain the same proportions to the back crotch extension. For example, if the length of the front crotch extension is 2 inches (5.1 cm) and the back crotch extension is 4 inches (10.2 cm), the ratio is 2:4, or simplified to 1:2. Therefore, if the front is lengthened by ¼ inch (6 mm), the back needs to be lengthened two times that, or ½ inch (1.2 cm). All changes made to the front will be one-half of those made to the back. And all changes to the back will be twice the front.

When shortening the length of the crotch extension for a fitted pant, the same rule applies. If you bring in the front crotch extension ¼ inch (6 mm), you will reduce the back length by twice that amount (½ inch [1.2 cm]). You can see how small changes can have a big impact on the fit and comfort of the rise. Make adjustments in small increments to start.

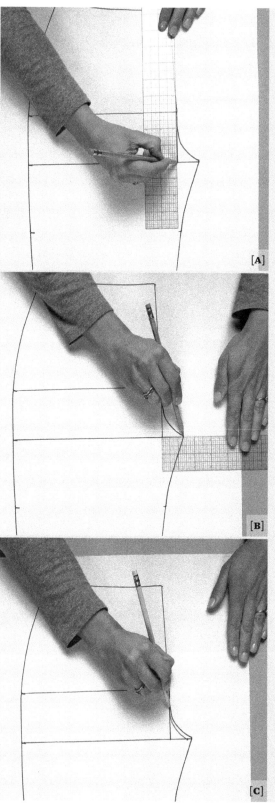

[A]

[B]

[C]

1
Trace the master pant pattern front and back onto drafting paper. Draw your hip-level and crotch-level guidelines.

2
Starting on the rise of your front pant pattern, draw a line perpendicular to your hip-level guideline down to the crotch-level guideline. Repeat for the back pant pattern [A].

3
Measure the distance from the vertical guideline to your crotch point on the crotch level guideline on both the front and the back. Figure out the ratio between the two, rounding to your nearest whole increment [B].

Refer to photo [C] for steps 4 and 5.

4
Adjust the front rise of the pant by bringing in the crotch point on the crotch-level guideline. Record the adjustment.

5
Redraw the shape of the rise from the crotch point to the waistline.

> **TIP**
>
> -
>
> *Fitting is absolutely necessary on a new master before proceeding to your fashion fabric.*

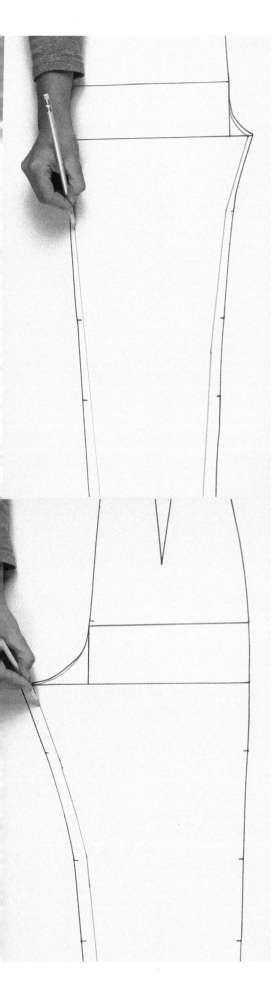

Refer to photo [**D**] *for steps 6–8.*

6

Decide how much you want to taper the base of the pant. Bring in the side seam and inseam by equal amounts.

7

Redraw the inseam from the crotch point to the base.

8

Redraw the side seam from the crotch-level guideline to the base.

Refer to photo [**E**] *for steps 9–12.*

[**D**]

9

Adjust the back crotch point on the crotch-level guideline the amount dictated by your pants ratio from step 3.

10

Adjust the base of the pant back the same amount as the front on both the inseam and the side seam.

11

Redraw the rise of your pant in a similar shape to your original rise, starting at the new crotch point and blending your hip-level guideline.

[**F**]

12

Redraw the back inseam from the crotch point to the base.

13

Redraw the back side seam from the crotch-level guideline to the base [**F**].

14

True your pattern: Your front inseam should match your back inseam length. In a fitted pant, there can be as much as ½" (1.3 cm) difference between your crotch point and knee. If there is a greater difference, adjust your crotch point down on the inseam with the longer measurement. Your side seam front measurement should match your side seam back measurement.

[**E**]

Changes for a Relaxed Pant

The changes to a relaxed pant can be slight or dramatic. Because the pant is more forgiving, so is the fitting process. It can be helpful to know what type of fabric you are working with as a more structured fabric will want a larger pattern adjustment. A fabric with great drape will need less of an adjustment due to its relaxed nature.

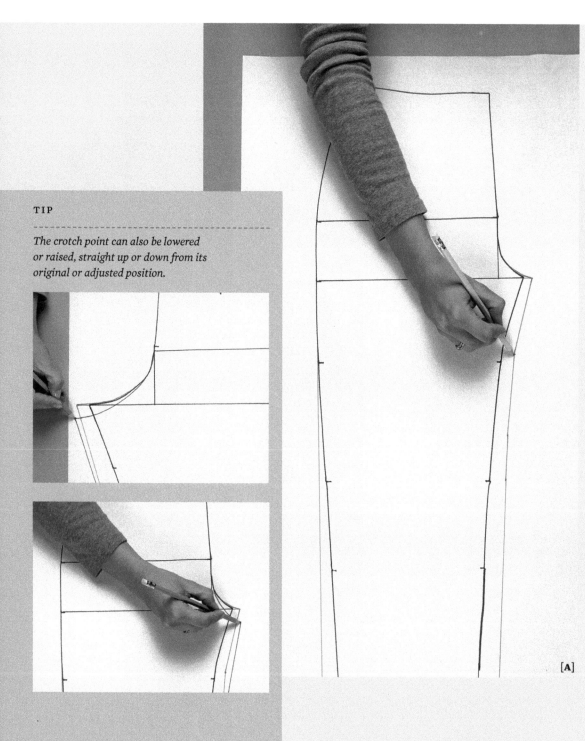

TIP

The crotch point can also be lowered or raised, straight up or down from its original or adjusted position.

Refer to photo [A] for steps 1–8.

1
Trace the master pant pattern front and back onto drafting paper. Draw your hip-level and crotch-level guidelines.

2
Starting on the rise of your front pant pattern, draw a line perpendicular to your hip-level guideline down to the crotch-level guideline. Repeat for the back pant pattern.

3
Measure the distance from the vertical guideline to your crotch point on the crotch-level guideline on both the front and the back. Figure out the ratio between the two, rounding to your nearest whole increment.

4
Adjust the front rise of the pant by extending out the crotch point on the crotch-level guideline. Record the adjustment.

5
Redraw the shape of the rise from the crotch point to the waistline.

6
Decide how much you want to widen the base of the pant to. Extend the side seam and inseam by equal amounts.

[A]

The same methods for drafting a skirt waistline and finish can be applied to pants and should be patterned before drafting other elements. Additional considerations should be made before drafting waistline finishes for pants. Where and what type of closure will the pant have? If you plan to have a fly front, then your waistband will need to be lengthened to accommodate the fly shield. A facing is a great low-profile way to finish the waistline and is more flattering with a side or back zipper.

It is common for pants to have a waistline that is much lower in the front than in the back. It is also common for pants to have both a waistband and a yoke. For example, jeans have a back yoke with a waistband on top. You can play with your waistline on pants with fewer limitations than with skirts because the pant legs alone help them hold their shape better.

TIP

You can create a yoke for your jean back using the same method as you would for a skirt yoke, only it does not wrap around to the front of the jean.

TIP

If you have a front dart in your pants, take half of the dart take-up off the center front rise and half off the back.

[B]

7
Redraw the inseam from the crotch point to the base.

8
Redraw the side seam from the crotch-level or hip-level guideline to the base.

Refer to photo [B] for steps 9–11.

9
Adjust the back crotch point on the crotch-level guideline the amount dictated by your pants ratio in step 3.

10
Redraw the rise of your pant in a similar shape to your original rise, starting at the new crotch point and blending your hip-level guideline.

11
Adjust the base of the pant back by the same amount as the front on both the inseam and the side seam.

12
Redraw the back inseam from the crotch point to the base.

13
Redraw the back side seam from the crotch-level guideline to the base.

14
True your pattern: Your front inseam should match your back inseam length. On a relaxed or full leg pant, the inseam length of the front and back should be equal. If there is a difference, adjust your crotch point down on the inseam with the longer measurement. Your side seam front should match your side seam back.

Pockets

Pants without pockets are missing an essential functional element. In fact, garments in general should have pockets. They are so useful! Garments without the traditional pocket details have a tendency to look homemade. It is easy to add pockets to any design and can really change the aesthetics of a garment. When well-done pockets are added to a garment, it looks more ready-to-wear and fashionable. Let these simple pocket-drafting instructions inspire more unique pockets.

There are very few rules to drafting pockets. Consider what the pocket is to hold and make it big enough, whether the pocket is to warm cold hands or hold your phone, keys, or lipstick. Make the pocket well supported. A pocket should be supported in a decent portion of the waistline so that when its contents weigh it down it does not swing around freely inside the garment.

Front Pockets

Use this pocket style on any pant. Play with the shape of your pocket opening, whether curved or straight. Try this style pocket in any garment— even skirts, dresses, and coats. It does not need to have a waistline seam, just a seamline that can support the pocket top.

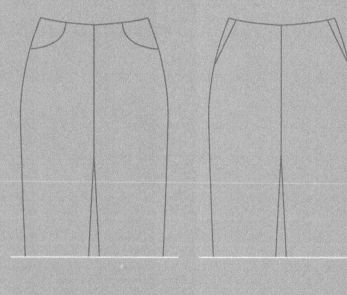

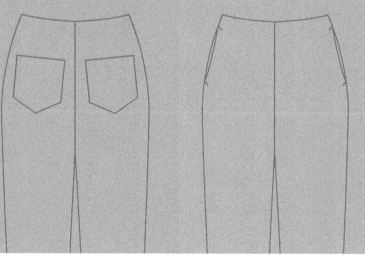

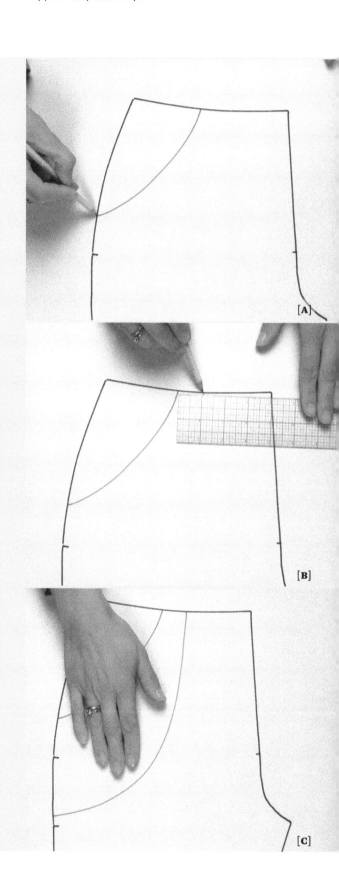

1
Trace your chosen master front pant pattern onto drafting paper. Make any changes to the waistline and waist finish.

2
Draw in the desired shape of the pocket opening, typically from the waist (below the waistband or yoke) to the side seam [A].

3
Make the waistline edge of the pocket width at least 1" (2.5 cm) closer to the center front as the pocket opening. The more waistline, the better [B].

4
Draw in the desired depth and shape of the pocket bag. Use your hand or the object the pocket is intended to hold as your guide [C].

5
Trace the shape of the pocket opening, the pocket bottom, and the portion of the waistline. This is your pocket bag front pattern. Draw the grainline parallel to the grainline of the pant. This will sit just behind the self fabric when worn [D].

[D]

[E]

[F]

6
Trace a second pattern piece that includes the pocket bottom, side seam, and the entire waistline in the pocket area. Notch where the pocket bag connects with the opening on the waistline and side seam. This is your pocket bag back pattern. Draw the grainline parallel to the grainline of the pant. This will sit closest to your body when worn [E].

7
Cut away the pocket opening as drawn in step 2 from the front pant pattern [F].

8
Label both the pocket bag front and the pocket bag back "Cut 2 of self fabric."

TIP

If your fashion fabric is bulky, create a pocket facing that is just a portion of your pocket bag back and extends at least 1" (2.5 cm) under your pocket opening. Both pattern pieces for the pocket bag front and back can be sewn out of lightweight lining, cotton, or pocketing fabric.

Patch Pockets

Patch pockets are common on the seat of jeans and as a breast pocket on button-down shirts. Reference the size and position of these pockets on your favorite pocketed clothing from your closet. Trace the shape of these onto drafting paper or measure and plot out a new pattern. Before sewing patch pockets onto the final garment, cut them out, press the raw edges under, and pin them in place on your fitting sample or your work in progress.

Pocket placement can really flatter or fail your backside!

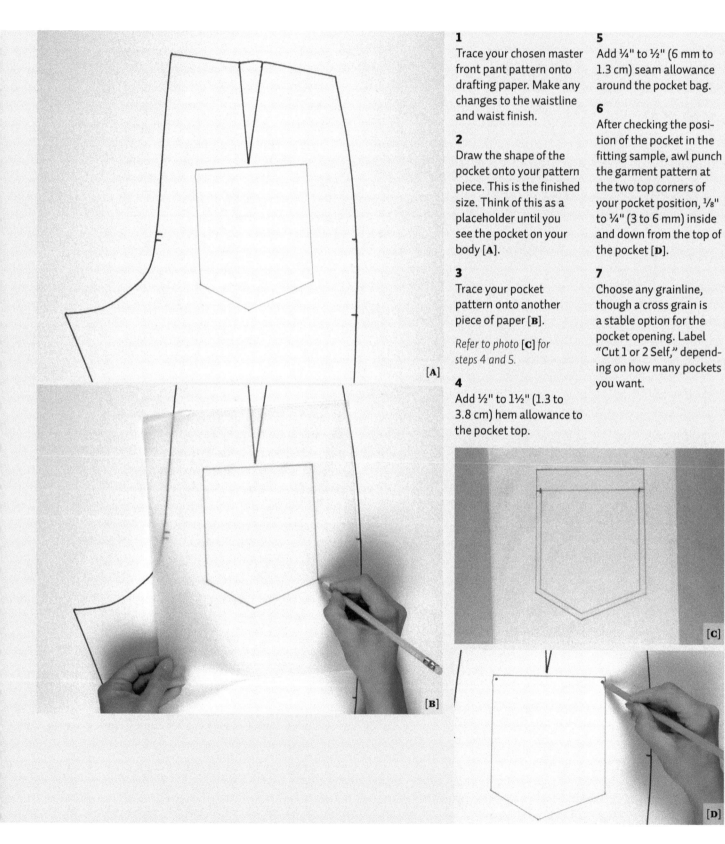

[A]

[B]

[C]

[D]

1
Trace your chosen master front pant pattern onto drafting paper. Make any changes to the waistline and waist finish.

2
Draw the shape of the pocket onto your pattern piece. This is the finished size. Think of this as a placeholder until you see the pocket on your body [A].

3
Trace your pocket pattern onto another piece of paper [B].

Refer to photo [C] for steps 4 and 5.

4
Add ½" to 1½" (1.3 to 3.8 cm) hem allowance to the pocket top.

5
Add ¼" to ½" (6 mm to 1.3 cm) seam allowance around the pocket bag.

6
After checking the position of the pocket in the fitting sample, awl punch the garment pattern at the two top corners of your pocket position, ⅛" to ¼" (3 to 6 mm) inside and down from the top of the pocket [D].

7
Choose any grainline, though a cross grain is a stable option for the pocket opening. Label "Cut 1 or 2 Self," depending on how many pockets you want.

Side Seam Pockets

Side seam pockets are slits in the side seam of a garment with a pocket bag inserted in between. They are the most discreet pockets. They absolutely must be sewn into the waistline of the garment; otherwise; they give new meaning to the term "saddlebags."

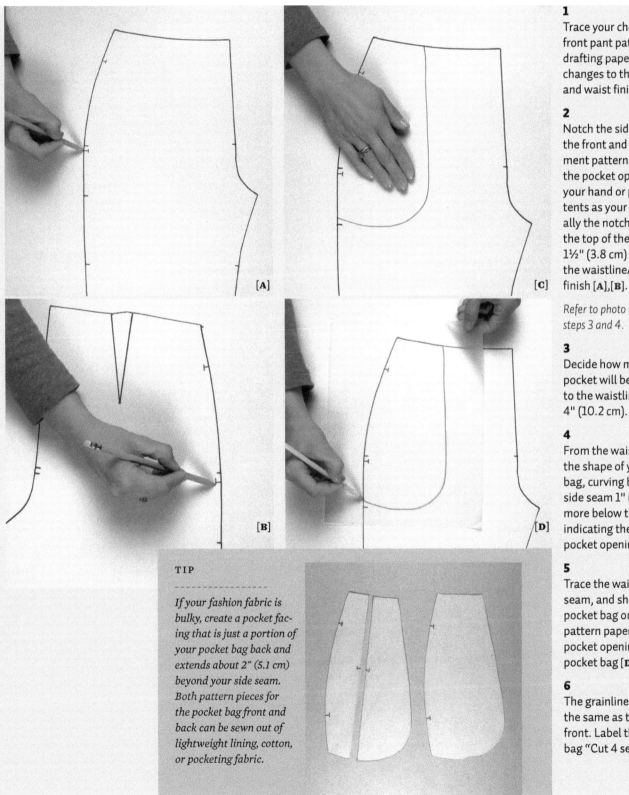

TIP

If your fashion fabric is bulky, create a pocket facing that is just a portion of your pocket bag back and extends about 2" (5.1 cm) beyond your side seam. Both pattern pieces for the pocket bag front and back can be sewn out of lightweight lining, cotton, or pocketing fabric.

1
Trace your chosen master front pant pattern onto drafting paper. Make any changes to the waistline and waist finish.

2
Notch the side seam on the front and back garment pattern to indicate the pocket opening. Use your hand or pocket contents as your guide. Usually the notch indicating the top of the pocket is 1½" (3.8 cm) down from the waistline/waistline finish [A],[B].

Refer to photo [C] for steps 3 and 4.

3
Decide how much of the pocket will be connected to the waistline, at least 4" (10.2 cm).

4
From the waistline, draw the shape of your pocket bag, curving back to your side seam 1" (2.5 cm) or more below the notch indicating the base of the pocket opening.

5
Trace the waistline, side seam, and shape of the pocket bag onto new pattern paper. Notch the pocket openings on the pocket bag [D].

6
The grainline should be the same as the garment front. Label the pocket bag "Cut 4 self or lining

Flared Pant

A flared pant adds any amount of volume starting at any level. Two iconic examples of a flared pant are the bootcut jean and the bellbottom. The bootcut has just a small amount of flare added below the knee, allowing the pant base to fit over boots.

The bellbottom has a significant amount of volume inserted at the thigh guideline.

This flare drafting method is fantastic and so versatile, and can be used on sleeves, dresses, skirts, and more. The beauty of this method is that it allows the garment to be fitted in certain areas and voluminous in others without adding seamlines.

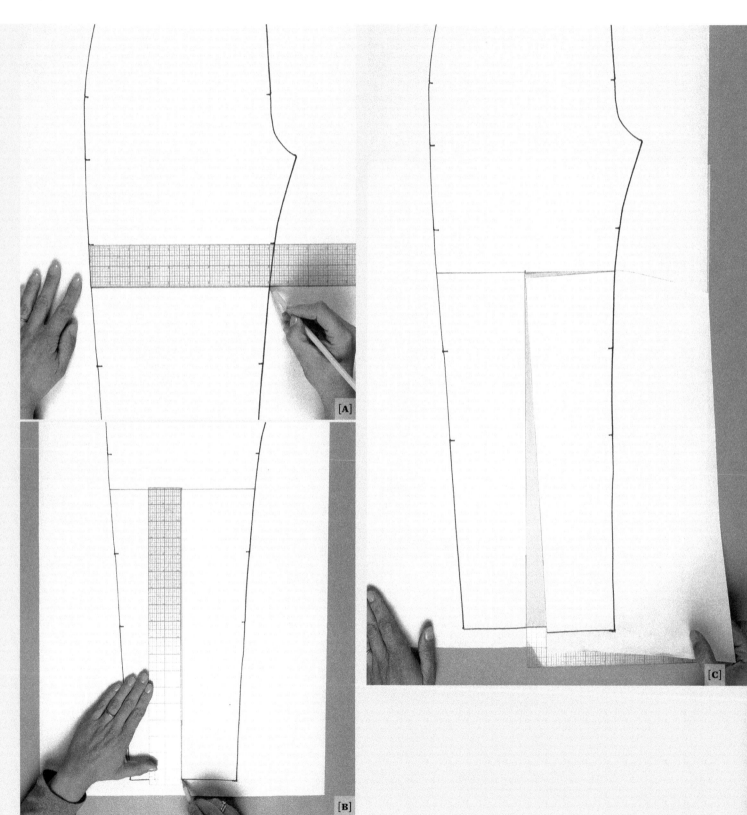

[A]

[B]

[C]

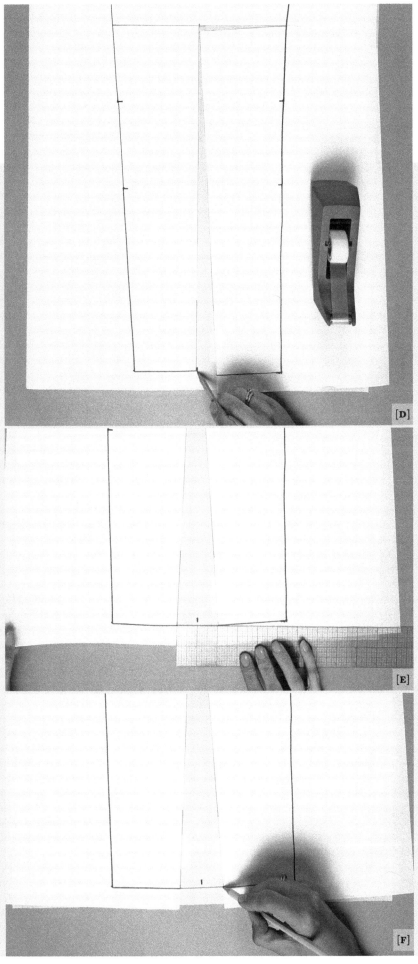

[D]

[E]

[F]

1
Trace your chosen master pant pattern onto drafting paper. Make any changes to the waistline and waistline finish, the length of the pant, and the pockets.

2
Decide on the level to begin the flare and draw a guideline perpendicular to your grainline. This is your flare-level guideline [A].

3
Find the center of this guideline. Draw an insertion line down to the base perpendicular to the flare-level guideline [B].

Refer to photo [C] for steps 4 and 5.

4
Cut the flare-level guideline up from the base and over to, but not through, the inseam.

5
Place another piece of paper underneath and pivot the pant from the inseam. Insert half of the desired volume.

6
Mark the original midpoint at the base [D]. Cut across the flare-level guideline to the side seam and insert the remaining half of the desired volume [E].

7
Connect the base across the insertions, curving slightly to remove any sharp angles [F].

8
Repeat for the back.

9
Mark the grainline the same as the original master pattern and label both the front and the back patterns "Cut 2 of self fabric."

Panel Pant

A panel pant is created by adding vertical stylelines. The stylelines can be drafted just on the front, just on the back, or both. The beauty of the panel pant is that you can get a very body-conscious fit through shaping the stylelines. Regardless of whether it is a relaxed or a fitted pant, the vertical seams are very flattering on the leg, as they lengthen and slim.

The position of the panel is generally centered over the leg. Finding the midpoints of the base, knee, thigh, and waist will give you a good reference point of where the styleline can be positioned.

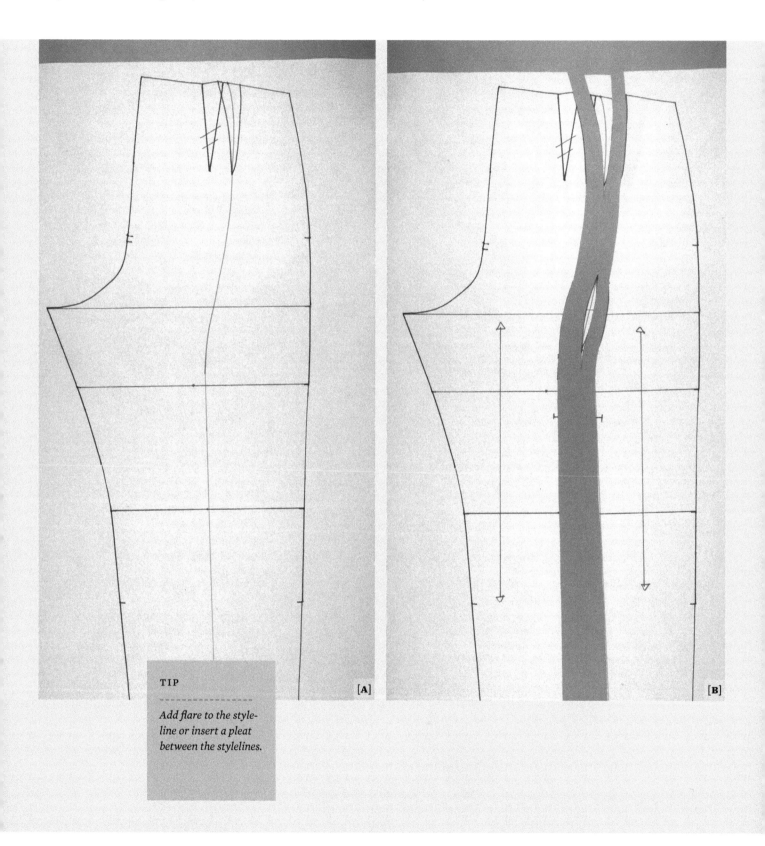

TIP

Add flare to the styleline or insert a pleat between the stylelines.

[A]

[B]

TIP
- -

Give the seam more contouring to better follow the curves of your body. For example, on your back crotch-level guideline shave ¼" (6 mm) off each side of the styleline, blending back to the vertical seam about 2" (5.1 cm) above and below the crotch-level guideline. Cut this away from your pattern to give you a snugger fit under the bum.

1

Trace your chosen master pant pattern onto drafting paper. Make any changes to the waistline, waist finish, and silhouette.

Refer to photo [A] for steps 2 and 3.

2

Find the midpoint of the base, knee, thigh, and waist. Use these as reference points to draw in a desired styleline.

3

If you have a front or back dart, move half of the dart take-up to each side of the styleline.

4

Draft a pocket, if desired, before separating your pattern pieces. See pages 146–149 for pocket instructions.

Refer to photo [B] for steps 5–7.

5

Place a notch across the styleline between the waist and the knee.

6

Cut the pattern pieces apart on the styleline, and cut away the dart take-up and any additional contouring.

7

Mark the grainline perpendicular to the base and label all pattern pieces "Cut 2 of self fabric."

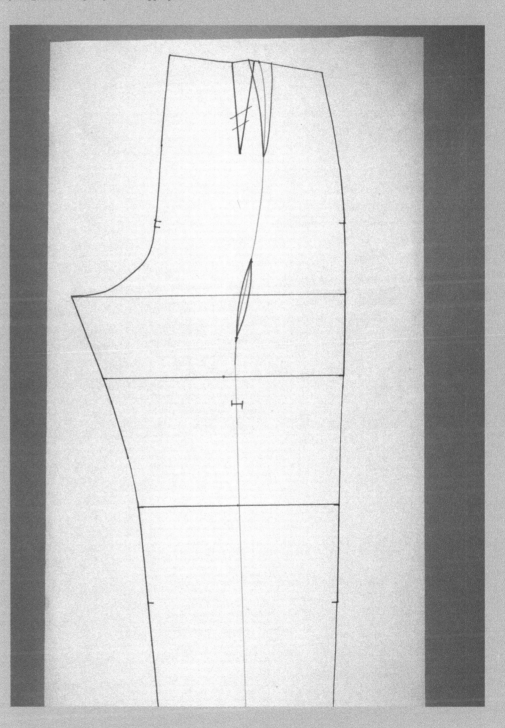

Pleated Pant

Pleats can be added to any garment much the same way as they were drafted in the skirt section, but it is uncommon for pleats to be added to a pant pattern in this way. In pants, pleats are generally added only to the front pattern and provide more fullness in the legs and not necessarily at the hem. If you have a dart in the pant front, the pleats should absorb it. Try to avoid inserting so much pleat volume that one pleat take-up overlaps with another pleat take-up.

Pleats will generally be more flattering if they are inserted at the midpoint of the waist so that they fall over the center of the leg. Pleats too close to the center front can begin to look like diapers with too much volume draping between the legs. Pleats too close to the side seam can get in the way of pockets.

There are two ways to add pleats. Drafting pleats to the base is very similar to how flare is added at the hem of a garment, but is done in reverse because the pleats will be added at the waistline. Drafting short pleats is very similar to how we patterned a flared pant but, again, in reverse. These pleats maintain the fit of the pant in certain areas and add volume only in some parts.

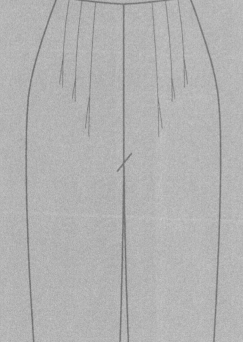

Pleats to the Base
Pleats to the hem add volume all through the leg, excluding the base.

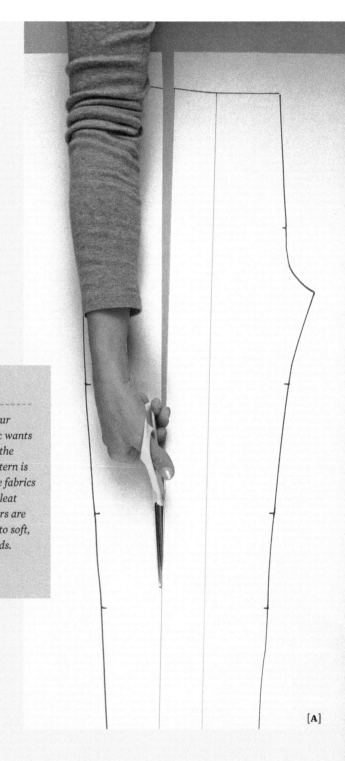

[A]

> **TIP**
>
> Make sure your fashion fabric wants to be pleated the way your pattern is drafted. Some fabrics hold a crisp pleat well and others are better suited to soft, unpressed folds.

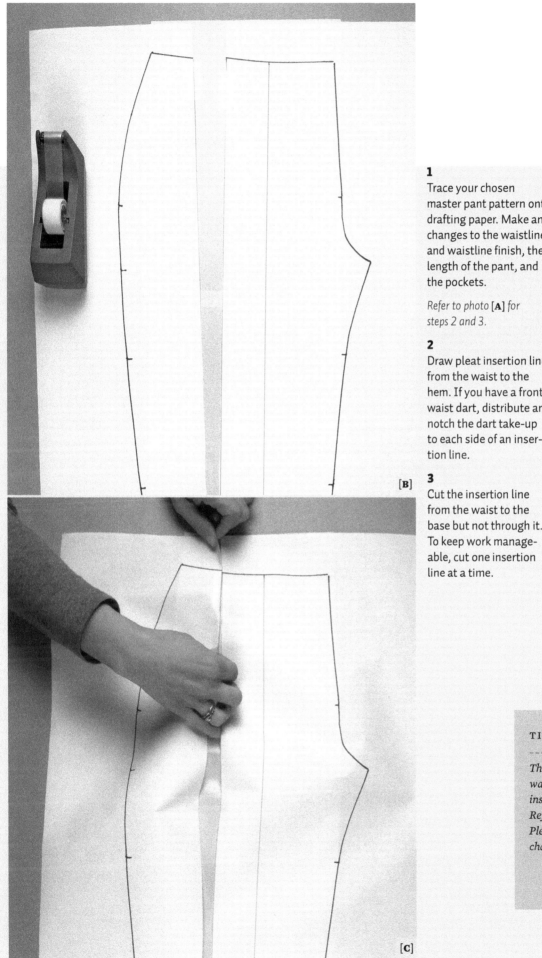

1

Trace your chosen master pant pattern onto drafting paper. Make any changes to the waistline and waistline finish, the length of the pant, and the pockets.

Refer to photo [A] for steps 2 and 3.

2

Draw pleat insertion lines from the waist to the hem. If you have a front waist dart, distribute and notch the dart take-up to each side of an insertion line.

3

Cut the insertion line from the waist to the base but not through it. To keep work manageable, cut one insertion line at a time.

4

Place another piece of paper underneath and insert as much or as little volume as desired. Secure with tape [B].

5

Fold your pattern the way you want your pleats to fold in the sewn garment. If you are using the pleat to absorb the dart take-up, be sure to fold out the total dart take-up, not just across the insertion line [C].

[B]

[C]

TIP

There are so many ways to fold out your insertions into pleats. Refer back to the Pleats in the Skirts chapter, page 46.

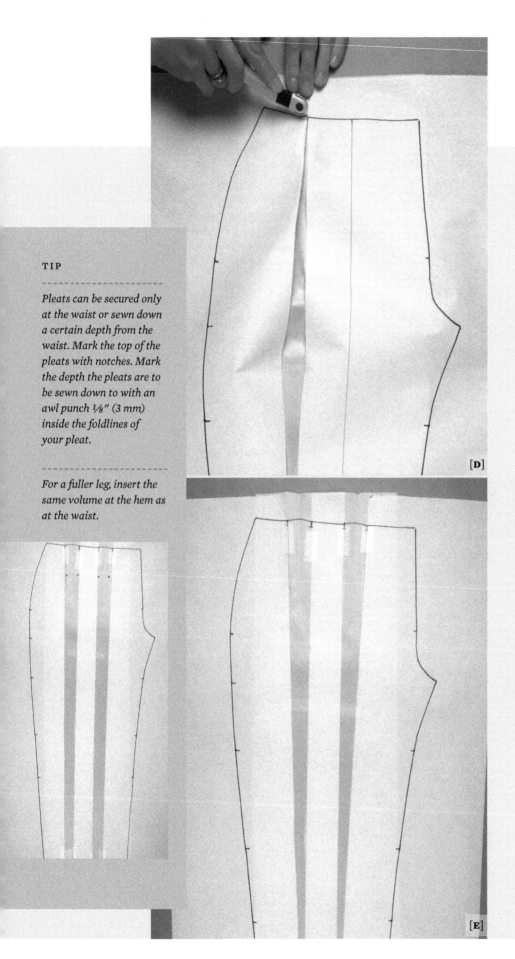

TIP

Pleats can be secured only at the waist or sewn down a certain depth from the waist. Mark the top of the pleats with notches. Mark the depth the pleats are to be sewn down to with an awl punch ⅛" (3 mm) inside the foldlines of your pleat.

For a fuller leg, insert the same volume at the hem as at the waist.

[D]

[E]

6
Trace the shape of your waistline through the folded paper. Unfold and draw in the shape across the insertion [D]. Notch along the insertion lines unless dart take-up was used, in which case you will use the dart legs as notches [E].

7
Repeat for all remaining insertion lines.

8
Draw grainline the same as the original master patterns and label both the front and the back patterns "Cut 2 of self fabric."

Short Pleats

Short pleats will keep your pant more fitted through the leg and provide extra volume only at the waist to the depth you decide.

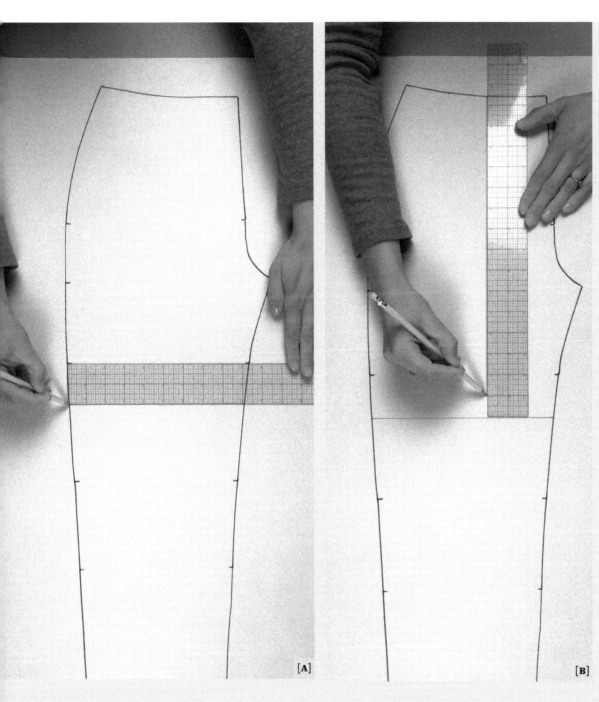

[A]

[B]

1

Trace your chosen master pant pattern onto drafting paper. Make any changes to the waistline and waistline finish, the length of the pant, and the pockets. In this draft, your waistline shape can get distorted, so be sure to trace it before making insertions.

2

Decide where you want your pant pattern to fit the same as your master pant pattern. This will determine how long your pleats will fall. Draw a horizontal guideline perpendicular to the grainline at this level. This is your pleat-level guideline [A].

3

Draw a vertical pleat insertion line from the waist to 1" (2.5 cm) above the pleat-level guideline [B].

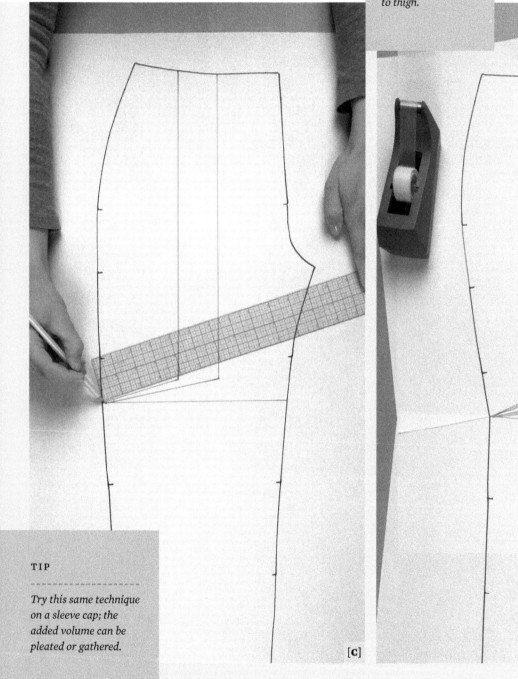

[C]

[D]

4

Connect the vertical insertion line to the side seam on the pleat-level guideline. If you have a front waist dart, distribute and notch the dart take-up to each side of one or more insertion lines [**C**].

*Refer to photo [**D**] for steps 5–7.*

5

Cut the angled pleat insertion line from the waist to the side seam. To keep work manageable, cut one insertion line at a time.

6

Place another piece of paper underneath and insert as much or as little volume as desired. Secure with tape.

7

Repeat for all insertion lines.

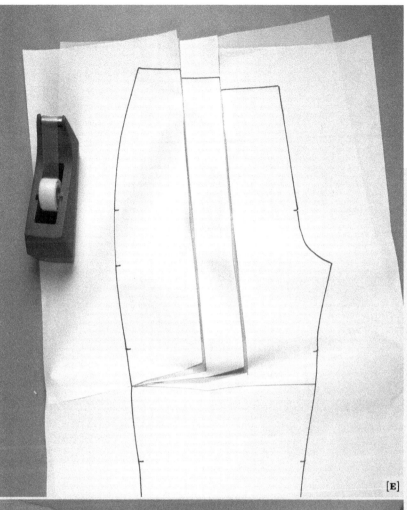

[**E**]

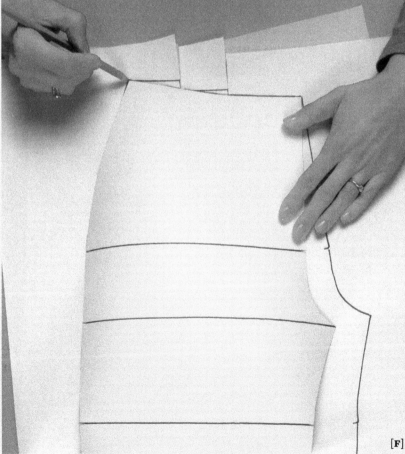

[**F**]

8

Fold your pattern the way you want your pleats to fold in the sewn garment [**E**].

If you are using the pleat to absorb the dart take-up, be sure to fold out the total dart take-up, not just across the insertion line. Because the insertion line is angled in this technique, it will affect your waistline shape. Use your traced waistline from step 1 as a guide when tracing the shape of your waistline through the folds [**F**].

9

Unfold and draw in shape across the insertions. Notch along the insertion lines unless dart take-up was used, in which case use dart legs as notches.

10

Draw the grainline the same as the original master patterns and label both the front and the back patterns "Cut 2 of self fabric."

Fly Front

A pant fly front should be placed on the straight section of the center front rise. Avoid building your zipper closure on a curved rise. There are two types of fly closures: a zipper fly and a mock zipper fly. Ready-to-wear uses a zipper fly and most commercial patterns use a mock zipper fly. Instructions for both patterns are included—draft the one you are the most comfortable sewing. Either a mock fly or a zipper fly can be patterned on a skirt.

Zipper Fly

A true zipper fly is what you will find on store-bought clothing. It has a seam along the fold of the center front, making it more stable, and sits under the center front by ¼ to ½ inch (6 mm to 1.2 cm). The pattern needs to be drafted with a right pant front and a left pant front because the pieces are patterned differently.

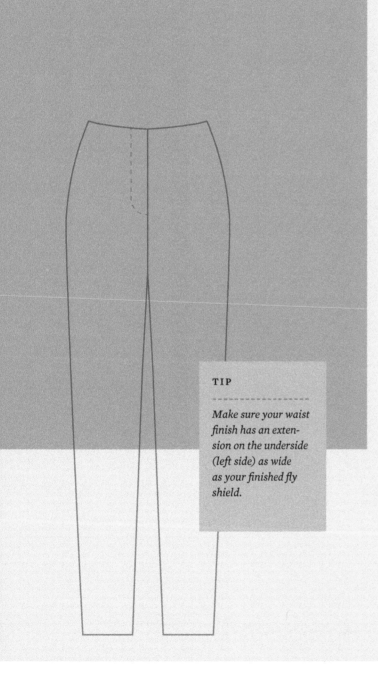

> **TIP**
>
> *Make sure your waist finish has an extension on the underside (left side) as wide as your finished fly shield.*

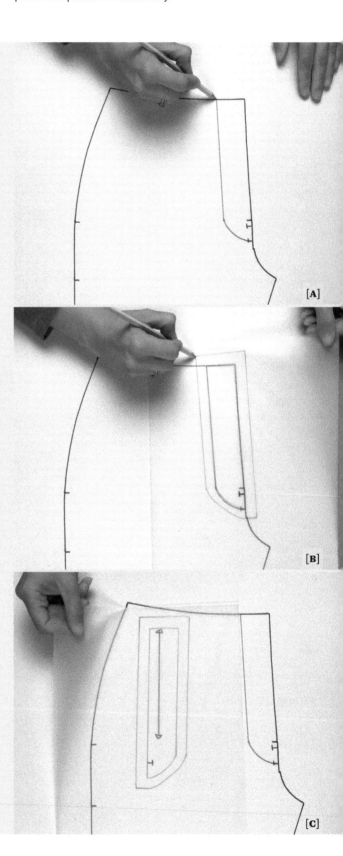

[A]

[B]

[C]

1

Trace a right and left front of designed pant pattern onto drafting paper.

Refer to photo [A] for steps 2–4.

2

Decide on the depth of the zipper from the waistline and notch. Make sure this length is straight. It may be a long length on a raised-waist pant or a very short length on a lowered-waist pant. This will indicate the functional opening of your fly and the length of your zipper.

3

Place another notch ½" to 1" (1.3 to 2.5 cm) below the depth of the fly; this will indicate the bottom of the fly shield that protects your body from your zipper.

4

On the right front pant, draw the shape of your zipper facing and shield. This will inform your topstitching and should also be at least as wide as your zipper.

5

On a new piece of paper, trace the shape of the zipper facing, add seam allowance all the way around, and flip the pattern over. This is a facing pattern piece and will be used to finish the right center front. Mark the

grainline parallel to the front rise and label "Cut 1 self fabric and interfacing" [B],[C].

6

Trace the shape of the zipper facing onto another piece of paper. Fold the new paper under along the center front rise and trace the entire shape with a tracing wheel. Open and draw in the shape [D]. Add seam allowance around the entire pattern piece. Notch the foldline at the top and bottom [E]. This is your fly shield and will get sewn to the left pant front. Mark the grainline parallel to the front rise and label "Cut 1 self fabric and interfacing."

7

On the left front pant, add an extension beyond the center front ¼" to ⅜" (6 to 10 mm) from the waistline to the bottom notch on the rise. You will then add seam allowance beyond that. This will allow your zipper to sit underneath your right front [F].

[D]

[E]

[F]

Mock Fly

A mock fly is generally what most home sew-ists are familiar with. The distance that the zipper sits under the folded center front can vary wildly depending on the width of your zipper tape. The front pant rise has an extension and is patterned the same for both the right and left pant front.

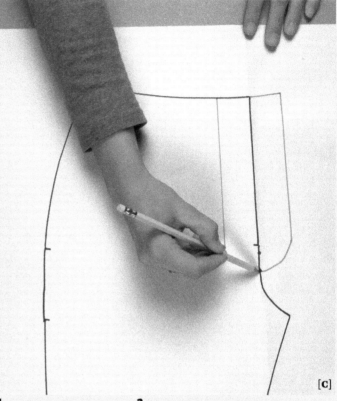

[A]

[C]

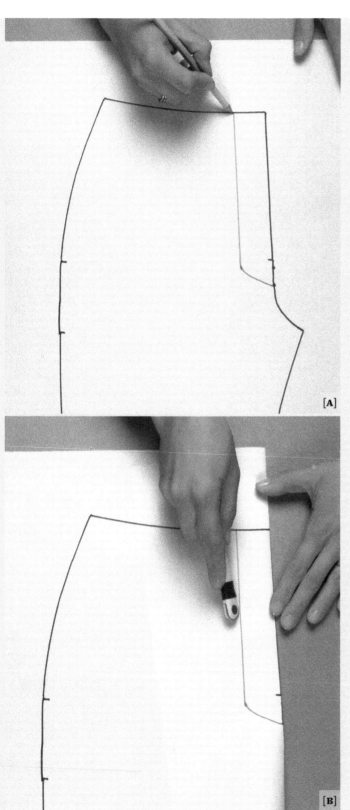

[B]

1
Design your garment.

Refer to photo [A] for steps 2–4.

2
Decide on the depth of the zipper from the waistline and mark it with an awl punch. Make sure this length is straight. It may be a long length on a raised-waist pant or a very short length on a lowered-waist pant. This will indicate the functional opening of your fly and the length of your zipper.

3
Place another awl punch ½" to 1" (1.3 to 2.5 cm) below the depth of the fly; this will indicate the bottom of the fly shield that protects your body from your zipper.

4
Draw the shape of your zipper facing and shield. This will inform your topstitching and should also be at least as wide as your zipper width.

5
Fold paper underneath at the center front and trace the shape of your zipper facing [B].

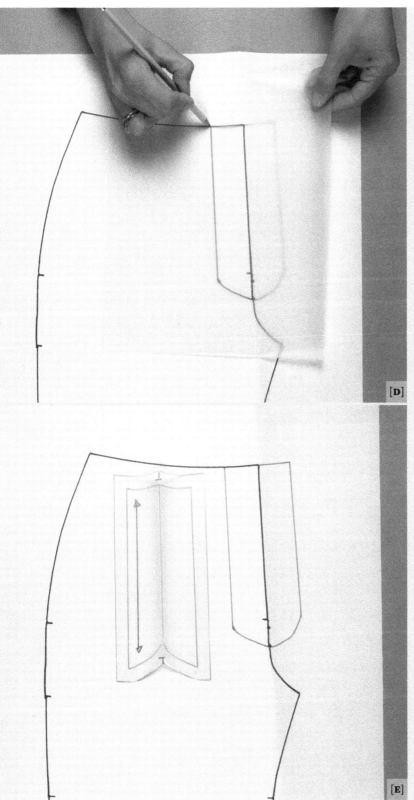

6

Unfold the paper and draw in the shape as an extension beyond the center front. This is your mock fly extension. Draw your grainline as on your pant master. Label the pant front "Cut 2 of self fabric" [**c**].

7

Trace the shape of the zipper facing onto another piece of paper [**D**]. Fold the new paper under along the edge of the zipper facing and trace the entire shape with a tracing wheel. Open and draw in the shape. Add seam allowance around the entire pattern piece. Notch the foldline at the top and bottom [**E**]. This is your fly shield and will get sewn to the left pant front. Mark the grainline parallel to the front rise and label "Cut 1 self fabric and interfacing."

[**D**]

[**E**]

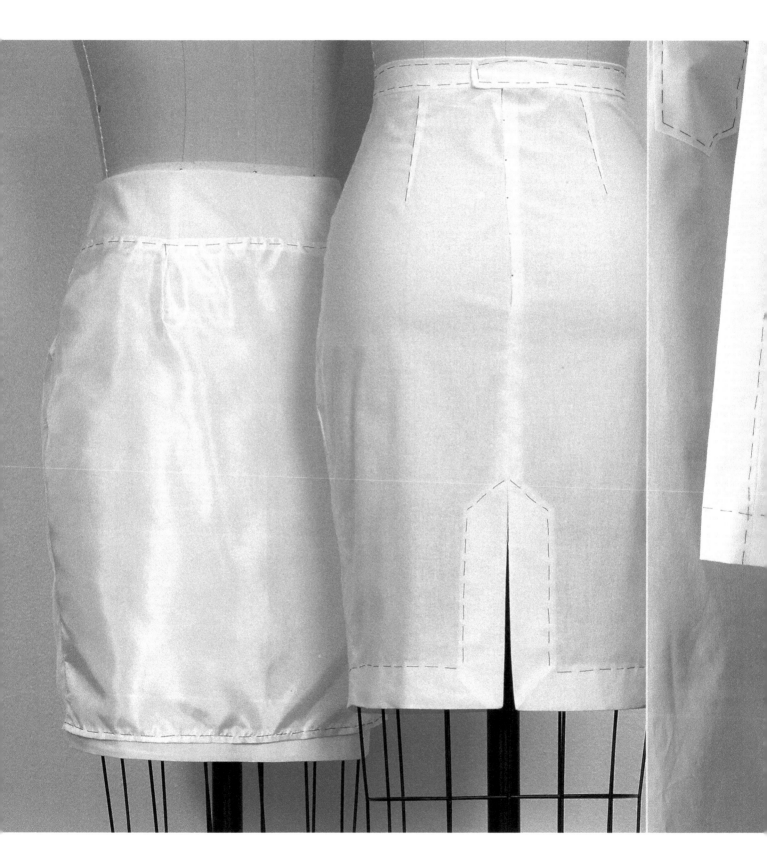

Finishing Details

The techniques in this chapter will offer you choices for finishing your garment in professional style.

Hem Finishes

At the base of every pattern, you need to decide on a hem finish. There is not one solution that fits every project. The three basic options are a narrow (or clean-finished) hem, a large single or double-fold hem, and a faced hem. Vary them to suit your project's needs.

Narrow Hem

A clean-finished hem has two folds. Generally, the first fold is ¼ inch (6 mm) and the second fold is ¼ to ½ inch (6 mm to 1.3 cm). This hem is great for the base of jeans, full skirts and dresses, blouses, and button-down shirts. It works well on lightweight fabrics and on hems that are slightly curved.

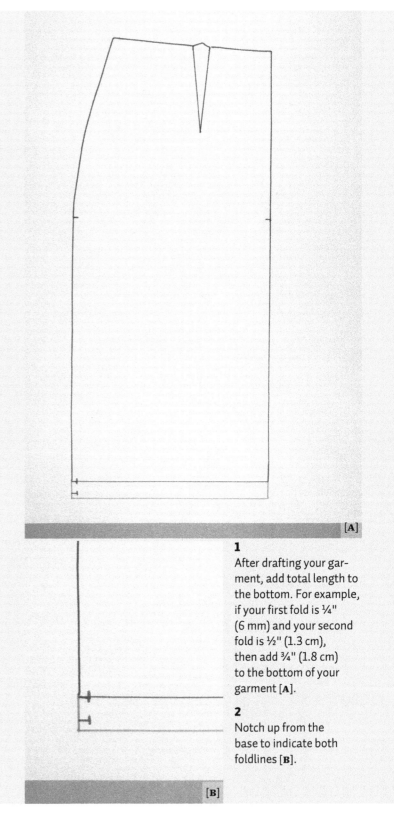

[A]

1
After drafting your garment, add total length to the bottom. For example, if your first fold is ¼" (6 mm) and your second fold is ½" (1.3 cm), then add ¾" (1.8 cm) to the bottom of your garment [A].

2
Notch up from the base to indicate both foldlines [B].

[B]

Large Hem

A larger hem can have a single or a double fold. A larger hem works well on garments that have a straight hem, where extra structure is desired or when attaching a lining.

A heavyweight fabric should be folded only once to avoid the hem becoming too stiff. Something lightweight and prone to fraying would do best with a double-fold hem. A large hem will not work on a garment with a curved hem.

Hem Facing

A faced hem is a lovely option for curved or shaped hems. It is great for asymmetrical hems, where the back hem is visible and it hangs below the front skirt hem length. A facing can be the same as the fashion fabric or a contrast, interfaced or not.

[A]

1
After drafting your garment, add the total desired hem allowance to the base. For example, if your first fold is ½" (1.3 cm) and your second fold is 1½" (3.8 cm), then add 2" (5.1 cm) to the bottom of your garment. Draw in each foldline [A].

2
Fold the hem up on the foldlines and trace the shape of the vertical seamlines through the folded paper [B].

3
Unfold the paper and draw the traced lines. Notch up from the base to indicate both foldlines [C].

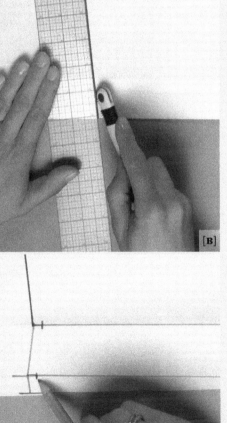

[B]

[C]

[A]

Refer to photo [A] for steps 1–4.

1
On your final garment design, add ¼" to ½" (6 mm to 1.3 cm) seam allowance to the base.

2
Decide how wide you want the hem facing to be, from 1" to 4" (2.5 to 10.2 cm).

3
Lay a piece of paper on top and trace the bottom hem and a portion of the side seams or vertical perimeter seams at the height that you want your facing to be.

4
Draw the upper edge of the facing to mimic the shape of the hem. This is your hem facing pattern piece.

5
Place notches between the seamlines or stylelines of facings and the base of the garment and the facing [B].

6
Mark the grainline and cutting instructions as for the garment [C].

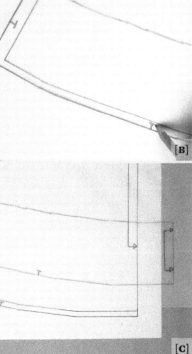

[B]

[C]

Slits and Vents

Slits and vents add mobility to sections of tight-fitting garments. They can be present on any vertical seam or styleline. A slit appears like a break in the seam above the hem. Common areas where you see slits are on seamlines of women's garments like a pencil skirt or tunic dress. The vent is different from a slit: the top layer appears like a break in the seam, while the other side lies underneath, making it a little more discreet. Vents are found in both men's and women's garments, and are common finishes on two-piece sleeve bases.

Slit

A well-done slit appears closed when it is in a relaxed or standing position, but allows for comfort when you walk or sit. The slit patterning will be the same on each side of a seam.

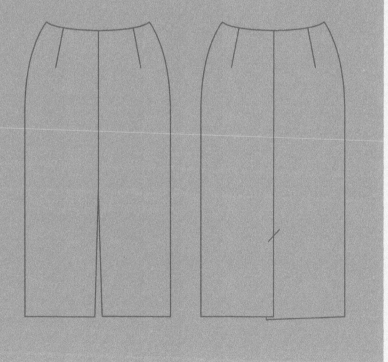

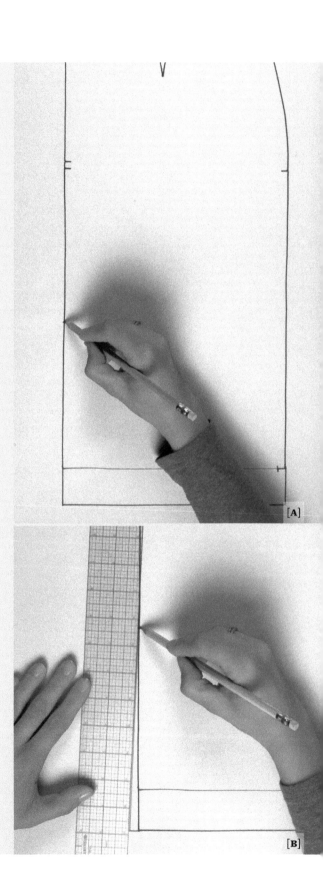

[A]

[B]

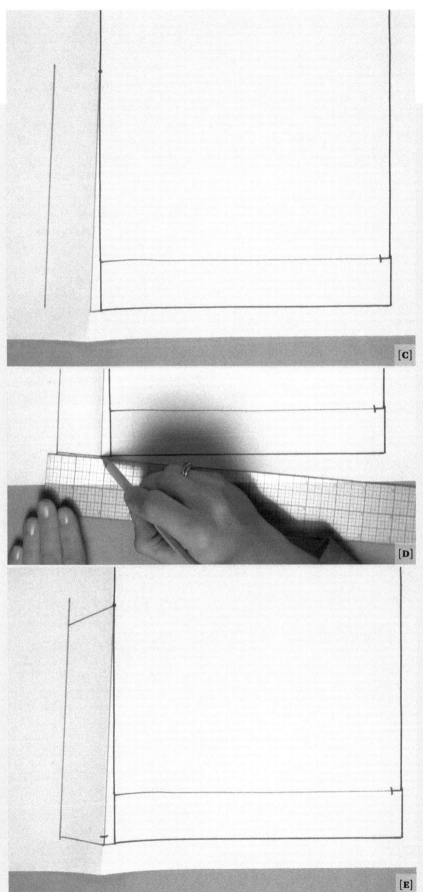

[C]

[D]

[E]

1

Decide which vertical seam you will draft your slit to and how long the slit will be. Mark the top of the slit with an awl punch. Add a large hem allowance to all pattern pieces. See page 166 for instructions [A].

Refer to photo [B] for steps 2 and 3.

2

Add an extension to the base of the vertical seam ¼" to 1" (6 mm to 2.5 cm). The shorter the slit and the straighter the garment, the smaller the extension should be. The longer and more fitted the garment, the larger the extension should be.

3

Connect the awl punch to the extended hem. This is your foldline.

4

From the foldline, measure the amount equal to the large hem allowance and draw a line that is parallel to the foldline [C].

5

Fold your paper pattern under on the foldline and trace the shape of the base of the skirt with a tracing wheel. Unfold the paper and draw the traced line. Notch on the foldline [D],[E].

6

Draw the top of the slit at a slight angle down from your awl punch. This will inform your topstitching line that holds the slit to each side of the seamline [E].

7

If you drafted your slit on the center front or back, then label your cutting instructions "Cut 2." If you drafted your slit to one side of a vertical styleline excluding the center front or back, repeat steps 1–5 on the other side of your vertical seam.

Vent

A vent has different pattern pieces for the upper and under portions. If the pattern piece is the same (such as a skirt back that is labeled "Cut 2"), then you'll have to make a right and a left pattern piece.

You will end up with "Cut 1 right back skirt" and "Cut 1 left back skirt." This does not apply to all pattern pieces, however; if you are placing a vent on a vertical styleline, for example, you will already have each side as separate pattern pieces. As is the

case with a two-piece sleeve, the upper vent will be drafted to the upper sleeve pattern piece and the under vent will be drafted to the under sleeve pattern piece.

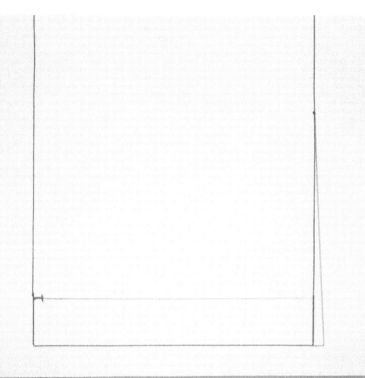

[A]

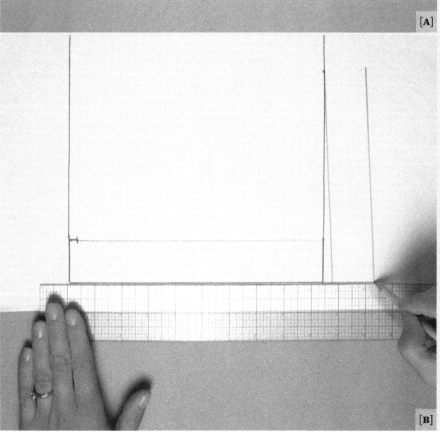

[B]

1
If needed, trace a right and left copy of the pattern piece that the vent will be drafted for.

Add a large hem to all pattern pieces.

2
Decide the height of the vent on the vertical styleline. Mark this with an awl punch on both sides of your pattern pieces.

3
Choose which pattern piece will be the upper vent. Follow the steps 2–6 for Slit on page 169.

This side is complete; set aside for later.

4
Draft the under vent. Add the same extension to the base of the vertical seam as the upper vent, from ¼" to 1" (6 mm to 2.5 cm). Connect the awl punch mark to the extended hem. This is your extension [A].

5
From your extension, measure the amount equal to the large hem allowance and draw a line that is parallel to the extension. This is your foldline. Connect your extension line to the new vertical line straight across the base [B].

[C]

[D]

TIP

- - - - - - - - - - - - - - - -

*Vents and slits
work best with a large
folded hem.*

6
Draw the top of your
under vent on the
same angle as your
upper vent [**C**].

7
Fold your paper under
on the foldline and trace
around the shape of the
vent top, the hem, and
the original styleline [**D**].

8
Unfold and draw in the
traced shape. Notch
on the foldlines at the
top and bottom of the
under vent [**E**].

[E]

Linings

There are two ways to line garments: hanging linings and bagged linings. A hanging lining falls freely from the top of the garment and is hemmed separately from the garment base. A bagged lining fully encloses the inside of the garment so no raw edges are visible. It gets sewn to the top and base of the garment.

If your design will be complex, with lots of seamlines/stylelines, it is better to trace your lining after you have drafted the waistline/neckline and the shape of the silhouette.

Hanging Lining

Hanging linings are the easiest to pattern and sew. They are great on skirts, pants, and dresses, but they are not appropriate for most sleeves.

[A]

[B]

> **TIP**
> -
> *If darts are in the garment, then the lining should pleat the dart take-up and be marked only with notches, excluding the awl punch indicating the dart point.*

Bagged Lining
Because a bagged lining will be sewn to the hem allowance, it needs a little bit of lengthwise ease so that it does not affect the drape of the garment. This is a great option for garments of many designs, except for pants.

1
Design your garment.

2
Trace the shape of each pattern piece to the finished base, or the hem's foldline, from the neck or waist finish down [A].

If this garment has a facing, then the lining starts below the facing. If the garment has a waistband, then the lining has the same waistline as the skirt or pant pattern piece.

3
Hem allowance is already included in the lining pattern. Notch up from the base ¼" (6 mm) to indicate the first hem fold and then another ¼" (6 mm) to indicate the second hem fold [B].

4
Do not add seam allowance to the base of the lining. Do add seam allowance to all other seamlines.

5
Mark the grainline and cutting instructions as for the garment.

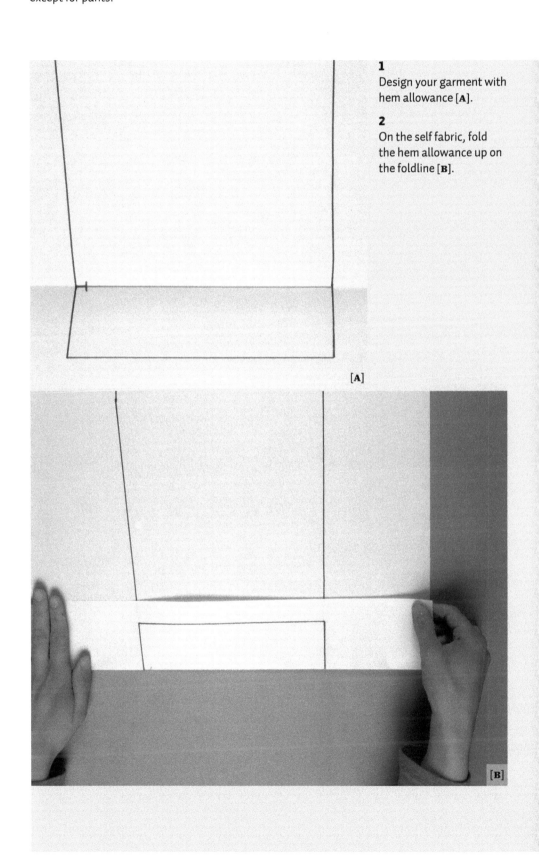

[A]

[B]

1
Design your garment with hem allowance [A].

2
On the self fabric, fold the hem allowance up on the foldline [B].

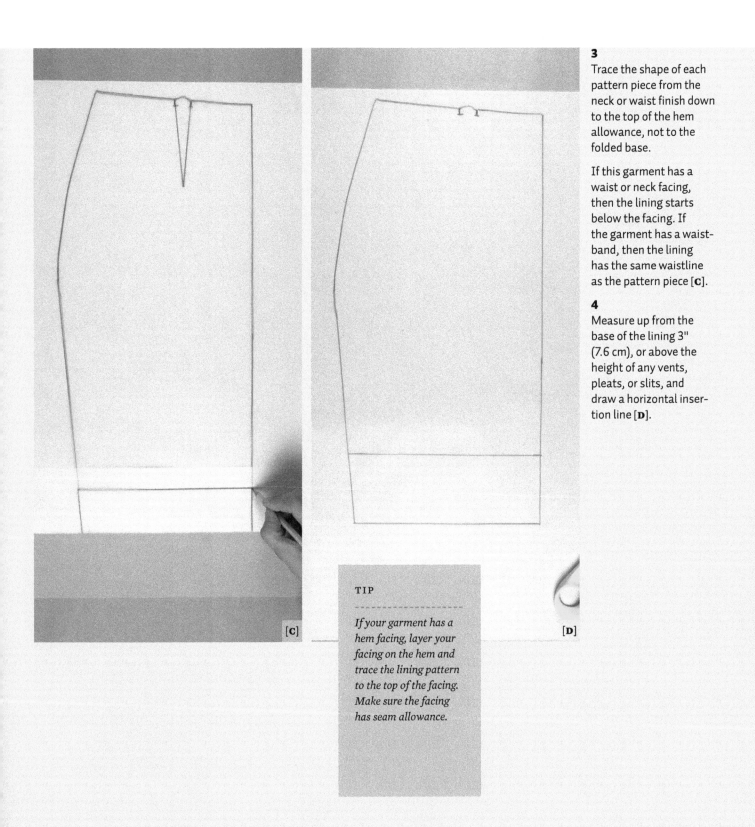

3
Trace the shape of each pattern piece from the neck or waist finish down to the top of the hem allowance, not to the folded base.

If this garment has a waist or neck facing, then the lining starts below the facing. If the garment has a waist-band, then the lining has the same waistline as the pattern piece [C].

4
Measure up from the base of the lining 3" (7.6 cm), or above the height of any vents, pleats, or slits, and draw a horizontal insertion line [D].

[C]

[D]

TIP

If your garment has a hem facing, layer your facing on the hem and trace the lining pattern to the top of the facing. Make sure the facing has seam allowance.

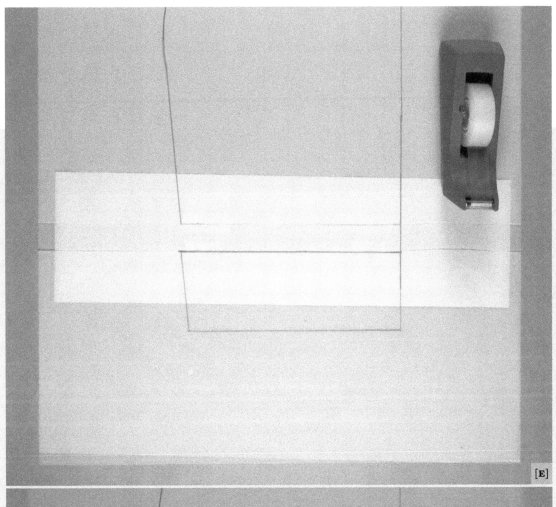

5
Cut the insertion line, place paper underneath the pattern, and insert 1" (2.5 cm). Use your grainline or center guideline to keep pattern in proper alignment [**E**].

6
Blend the vertical styleline across the insertion [**F**].

7
Mark the grainline and cutting instructions the same as the garment. Be sure to add seam allowance to all pattern pieces, including the base of the garment and the lining.

[**E**]

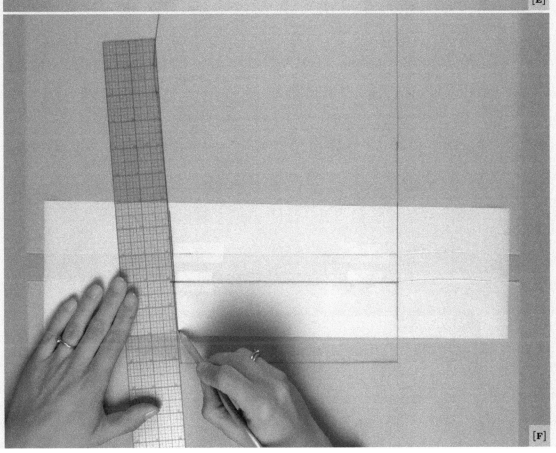

[**F**]

ABOUT THE AUTHOR

Sara Alm started sewing dresses at age six, and she has never looked back. Since graduating from the Apparel Arts patternmaking program in 2005, Sara has worked as a patternmaker, designer, and sewing instructor at Apparel Arts. Sara is the co-author of Famous Frocks: Patterns and Instructions for Recreating Fabulous Iconic Dresses—10 Patterns for 20 Dresses In All!

Sara is the instructor for eight Craftsy Classes: Fitting Sewing Patterns: Essential Techniques; Mastering Construction: Sleeves; Mastering Construction: Collars and Closures; Mastering Construction: Facings and Linings; Mastering Construction: Foundation Techniques; Mastering Construction: Zippers and Waistbands; The Essential Guide to Sewing With Sheers; *and* Inside Vogue Patterns: Tracy Reese V1397.

Resources

DRAFTING SUPPLIES
www.fashionsuppliesinc.com
www.sewtrue.com
www.wawak.com
www.apparelcitysf.com
www.amazon.com

BLOGS AND MAGAZINES
www.thecuttingclass.com
www.grainlinestudio.com
www.seamwork.com
Threads
Vogue Patterns

CLASSES
Apparel Arts
www.craftsy.com

Awl
A small tool that is used for making holes in fabric to mark dart points, pivot points, intersecting seamlines, and pocket placement. There are sewing-specific awls, but awls from the hardware store work just fine as well.

Awl punches
Marks or holes made by an awl in fabric. Awl punches also refer to the drawn dots on your pattern that indicate where you should make an awl punch when marking the fabric.

Bias grain
An alternative for laying out and cutting fabric. It is diagonal to the selvedge edge, or 45 degrees from the original grainline. Something cut on the bias grain has more drape and give because the fabric's weave is more lattice shaped around the circumference of the body.

Cross grain
When a pattern piece is cut with the center front or back perpendicular to the grainline and the selvedge edge.

Double notch
Two notches used side by side. Usually a double notch is used to indicate the center back of a pattern piece and/or the base of the zipper opening, though they can be used to guide how pattern pieces of a more complicated design connect together.

Ease
The amount a garment is bigger than our bodies. A very relaxed garment will have many inches of ease, whereas a very fitted garment will be only slightly bigger than the body.

Extension
Extra volume added to the perimeter of the pattern.

Fly shield
A piece of fabric often as wide as the zipper that sits between the body and the zipper. It protects the skin from the zipper teeth.

Gorge point
The intersection of the seam where the collar meets the lapel.

Grainline
How a pattern should be laid out on the fabric when cutting. The straight grainline of the fabric is parallel to the selvedge edge running the length of the fabric. A pattern piece cut on the straight grain will have its center front and back running in the same direction as the selvedge of the fabric.

Insertion
Extra volume added to the interior of the pattern, by cutting through the pattern and adding more width or length.

Insertion lines
Drafting lines that are cut to allow for more volume in a pattern.

Muslin
A plain-weave cotton fabric that is inexpensive. It comes undyed or bleached. It is a great fabric to use when testing the fit of a garment. Any fabric used to test the fit of a garment is referred to as a muslin or toile.

Notch
A small cut on the perimeter of the fabric pattern piece. A notch is used to show which pattern pieces connect to each other, where dart legs are, what seam allowance a pattern was cut with, and where seamlines match up to other pattern pieces. A notch can be drawn on a paper pattern piece in several ways; it is sometimes shaped like the letter T, or it can look like a small triangle above or below the seamline. It can be cut to the same shape in fabric or can be just a small snip about ¼ inch (6 mm) deep from the raw edge of the fabric.

Notcher
A tool that is used to make small notches in paper patterns to indicate a guideline as it falls on the perimeter of the pattern piece. It functions similar to a paper hole punch.

Oak tag paper
A paper that is heavy weight and can stand up to the abuse of tracing around its perimeter multiple times. It lies or hangs flat. It is great for use with master patterns or patterns that you want to cut out of fabric again and again. Office file folders are made of the same material. Substitute any heavyweight paper for your use.

Off-grain
When something is not cut on an accurate grainline. The result will be a finished garment that does not hang properly on the body.

Pattern hooks
Small hanger hooks attached to a T-shaped bar by a string. They are designed to hold your patterns on a closet rod or garment rack.

Roll line
The foldline of a collar with a stand. A collar with a stand "stands" above the neckline and folds at the roll line to its "fall."

Stylelines
Additional seamlines designed into a garment. They can be seamlines for seamlines' sake, or they can be used to replace darts and other shaping.

True pattern
To make sure that seams to be sewn together are the same length and that the notches match across the seam. Also that the shape of a pattern makes a smooth transition across a seam. For example, the shape of a neckline should not have undesired points or valleys across the shoulder seam.

Underbust
Horizontal guideline below and parallel to the bust guideline. Measure down from the bust apex to your rib cage to determine how far below the bust guideline it should be. Notice that there can often be more waist dart take-up on that guideline.